Rising Up From the Blood: A Legacy Reclaimed— A Bridge Forward

The Autobiography of Sarah Washington O'Neal Rush
The Great-Granddaughter of Booker T. Washington

D0878687

Rising Up From the Blood: A Legacy Reclaimed— A Bridge Forward

The Autobiography of Sarah Washington O'Neal Rush
The Great-Granddaughter of Booker T. Washington

By Sarah Washington O'Neal Rush

With Yvonne Rose

Solid Rock Book Publishing
San Leandro, California

Rising up From the Blood: A Legacy Reclaimed—A Bridge Forward
Published by:
Solid Rock Book Publishing
San Leandro, California
Washingtonwisdom@btwen.org
ExtraordinaryLegacy.net

Sarah Rush, Publisher / Editorial Director
Yvonne Rose/Quality Press, Production Coordinator
Printed Page, Cover & Text Layout

Dedication

I dedicate this book to my mother; Agnes Louise Washington O'Neal—my number one fan. Though we took the long way around, I would have never become the person I am today without her. I miss her deeply. I especially miss having her around in the midst of my accomplishments. The pride in her facial expressions was priceless. I also miss her whenever there is a major news event that I know would have broken her resistance to watch television... the election of our first Black President, Barack Obama, would have surely been one of those times. I am certain that by now she would have read everything published in good taste about our First Lady, Michelle Obama. Every day I find myself becoming more and more like all that was special about her. I believe she continues to watch over me from above. I know I will see her again...one day. Thank you Momma.

Acknowledgements

First and foremost my deepest thanks goes to my husband, **Anthony "Tony" Rush**. Without your relentless patience, love, and support, this 12-year project could not have been completed. To my children, **Mario, Regarah, and Iesha**, I thank you all for your unconditional love, for breaking destructive cycles, and for your inspiration. To my little hearts, my grandchildren, **Amari Louise, Saniya Olivia**, and **Velez Dante**, just the fact that you all have shown signs that you admire me, is more than enough to inspire me.

To **Lillian "Cissy" White and Patsy Lockhart**, my friends and fellow California Berries, thanks for advising and encouraging me, and for the much needed fun along the way! To **Nikki Thomas**, for your beautiful spirit, your encouragement, and for always exposing my work to your listening audience. To my **Allen Temple family**, especially **Pastor Smith, Jr., Pastor Jacqueline Thompson, Pastor Smith, Sr., Reverend Donald Miller, and Mary Ellen and Gerald Jones**—words cannot express what you all mean to me, and what you have taught me by your examples, about our Lord and Savior, Jesus Christ.

To **Reverend Harry Louis Williams, III**, for saying to me during our first one-on-one conversation, "If you could see what I see sitting on the other side of this table…," for shining a light on my potential, and most of all for encouraging, assisting, and inspiring me to pick up where I left off on this manuscript.

Last, but clearly not least, to **Mary B. Morrison**, thank you for sending me to Quality Press and believing in me enough to introduce me to a literary genius, **Tony Rose,** and his gifted wife, **Yvonne Rose** who worked with me on this book. Without the **Roses**, this project would not have come to fruition. My sincere thanks belongs to each of you!

Table of Contents

Foreword

Sarah Washington O'Neal Rush is as close to American Royalty as one can get. Her Great-Grandfather, Booker T. Washington, saved the lives of millions of African American people. Near the turn of the 19th century a man who had once been a slave, rose to become one of the greatest leaders America has ever produced. He told America that they didn't need to systematically kill off African Americans, but rather that African Americans could be of service to them in technology and agriculture. On July 4, 1881 Booker T. Washington founded Tuskegee Normal, which became Tuskegee Institute, and was later named Tuskegee University.

Many years had passed when Sarah knew nothing about the true meaning of her heritage; but finally everything came full circle when she realized the power of her legacy. Sarah had an epiphany when she visited Tuskegee University for the first time. For Sarah, the veil of ignorance was lifted that day. Shortly thereafter, she became clear about her purpose and began to embark upon her intended journey in life.

For decades, as a child, a teen and a young adult, Sarah struggled with many insecurities brought upon her by unstable living circumstances; and she carried those insecurities into adulthood. Little did she know that the time spent falling and failing could only serve as a stepping stone to a future that would help her own children and grandchildren, and the numerous youth that she would encounter.

Booker T. Washington fervently believed that you "Lift yourself up by lifting others up." His principles surrounding the importance of education, although unbeknownst to Sarah while she was growing up, had obviously trickled down through her bloodline and caused a thirst to learn all she could. Her Great-Grandfather would be very proud as Sarah discovered and shared, openly and honestly, the many obstacles that even a "blue-blood" must challenge head on.

Although Sarah spent much of her youth seeking a solution for her personal discontent, she now, with the help of her ancestors, is determined to accept her challenge to become a true leader and follow in the footsteps of her Great-Grandfather, Booker T. Washington, and bring his words, with her courage, to today's youth.

As the youngest Great-Grandchild, Sarah intends to hold fast to her heritage and reclaim her legacy, which began with the strongest woman in the bloodline. Booker's mother Jane was a slave who gave birth to three slave children. Sarah hails her Great-Great-Grandmother as a true embodiment of courage and womanhood; and honors Jane's strength and perseverance as the foundation for Booker's success.

Sarah Washington O'Neal Rush has valiantly taken the baton that was passed down to her through the lineage of her Great-Great-Grandmother Jane, through her Great-Grandfather Booker T. Washington, through her Grandfather Ernest Davidson Washington and through her mother Agnes Louise Washington.

Rising up from the Blood: A Legacy Reclaimed—The Autobiography of Sarah Washington O'Neal Rush, The Great-Granddaughter of Booker T. Washington is the honest true story of an unassuming child who would learn to take poverty for granted. For years, the quietness of her lineage hindered Sarah's potential. For Sarah, there had been no hint that she had aristocratic, blue blood flowing through her veins. This is Sarah Washington O'Neal Rush's remarkable true story…of her awakening!

—Tony Rose, Publisher, Amber Books
   NAACP Image Award Winner for Outstanding Literature

Preface

My great-grandfather, Booker T. Washington, was the inspiration for this book. He was born a slave on a plantation in Franklin County, Virginia. As was common to slaves, there were no records of his exact date of birth. The best evidence available suggests, April 5, 1856.

As a former slave, he worked tirelessly to become the most influential African-American of his era. He had specific ideas regarding the best ways for former slaves, and their descendants, to improve their lives and, on a larger scale, improve their communities. With over 10 million followers, Booker T. Washington was a successful teacher, author, political figure, and orator. His famous speech, the Atlanta Exposition Address, otherwise known as the Atlanta Compromise Speech, was an agreement between Black leaders and Southern White leaders in which Southern Blacks would work meekly and submit to White political rule, while Southern Whites guaranteed that Blacks would receive basic education and due process in law. What many misunderstand is, this was not Booker T. Washington selling out, but rather, it was a strategy for getting ahead.

His autobiography, "Up From Slavery," was published in 1901. It was a best seller that was (and continues to be) inspiring, it was translated into over 17 different languages, and has never been out of print. The book chronicles over fifty years of his life: from slave, to schoolmaster, to the most dominant voice of southern race relations. Throughout the text, Booker T. Washington stresses the importance of education on the Black population as a reasonable tactic to ease race relations in the South.

Booker T. Washington promoted self-help and manual skills as opposed to liberal arts. He believed that, after slavery, Black Americans would be able to contribute and be accepted more easily and significantly in the wider national community through this approach. He argued that it helped African-Americans immediately and did not threaten the White community. He garnered a significant degree of support among both groups, stating "A race, like an individual, lifts itself up by lifting others up."

Introduction

I am proud and honored to be the great-granddaughter—the last born grandchild of the fourth generation of Booker T. Washington. The day I went to my first "Washington" Family Reunion in Tuskegee in 1996, I had no idea how dramatically my reality was about to change. After it was over I felt as though I had been reborn. When I first stepped foot on the campus of the renowned Tuskegee University, something magical happened. Once I returned home, I had an epiphany and was immediately inspired to improve my life.

Prior to the day of our family reunion, I was going in the wrong direction, and by the time I was sixteen I had become a lost soul, confused about life. I didn't realize from whence I came, or understand that I had been delegated by my ancestors to pass the baton to thousands of young people who needed to turn their obstacles into opportunities.

Even the assumption that I was ordinary as a child was a step-up from what I would have anticipated when the inevitability of poverty was knocking at my door. For me, there had been no silver spoons, no family highlights, no special privileges, or opportunities, and few prideful moments—despite the fact that my great-grandfather had founded Tuskegee Normal School (later Tuskegee Institute, and today Tuskegee University).

Booker T. Washington knew almost nothing of his ancestry. In his autobiography, "Up From Slavery", he wrote: "In the slave quarters…I heard whispered conversations among the colored people of the tortures which the slaves, including, no doubt, my ancestors on my mother's side, suffered in the middle passage of the slave ship while being conveyed from Africa to America." He did not know who his father was, but he heard rumors that he was a White man who lived on a nearby plantation, who most likely raped his mother, Jane, a slave woman.

As a slave, my great-grandfather had been deprived of education. His thirst to learn was overwhelming. One of his slave duties as a little boy was to walk behind his master's children to school as he carried their books. Once they went in the classroom, he would hang around to listen to what the teacher was saying. He'd run away before getting caught. At that time, a slave learning to read or write was a crime—a crime punishable by death. In describing his desire for an education, he said, "I believe that getting into a schoolhouse would be like arriving into paradise." What if more of our children felt like that today? When he was a child in the late 1800's, Booker T. Washington knew what the slave masters knew—that knowledge was power. That fact is unchanged today, over a century later.

His education, and the continuing education of other African-Americans who had risen up from slavery, along with their future lineages, would become Booker T. Washington's greatest inspiration. This was the legacy that he would endow upon his own children and their descendants. However, when it came to learning my own family history, the ball was dropped before it got to me.

Before this reunion, most of what I learned about the incredible achievements of my ancestors occurred in sermons in the Black church. Preachers would speak out about our foreparents in order to build our self-esteem. They magnified what they did for us collectively. That alone was enough to temporarily stir up deep and prideful emotions inside of me, as well as in the rest of the congregation. More often than not, I fought back tears as I listened to the stories about those who came before us, who looked like us, and who broke down barriers for us so that we could live better. I knew that their blood was my blood.

Another Sunday drew to a close, and the new week was on the horizon, because I didn't have a strong foundation—the inspirational feelings would soon dissipate into the storms of destructive thoughts competing for space in my mind. Sadly, this is the reality for so many today. There is no question that the foundation our ancestors started for us, is now very weak. For a long time, my life was evidence of its weakness. Today, I am pleased to be in a place that empowers others to rise above the storms of life.

It wasn't until I arrived in Tuskegee, Alabama as an adult, in the South for the first time in my life, that I would bear witness to my foundation—a foundation that was there all along. That's when I began to live on purpose. It is also why I now feel a burning obligation to share my story—hoping that I can encourage others to draw strength from their own story, their mistakes, their lessons, their victories, and their history—all in order to inspire and teach someone else how to succeed.

It is not my intention to offend anyone in the writing of my story, but instead to tell from my perspective, of the significant events which shaped my life. The following chapters are intended to contribute to the work that continues. It is my hope that this book will empower others to change unhealthy mindsets, increase levels of self-worth, and instill a healthy sense of self-love and self-respect within. This should overflow to others daily.

With the year 2015 on the horizon, marking 150 years since the end of chattel slavery in America, I believe the release of *Rising Up From the Blood*, is not only timely, but it is divinely ordered. Now I invite you to come down in the trenches, and journey with me as I share my story of rising up from the blood and reclaiming my legacy.

"One's positon in life is not measured by the heights which they have attained, but by the depth's from which they have come."

—Booker T. Washington

What I've Learned from my Great-Grandfather's life

God is no respecter of persons, thus I should not be either. It's not my title that matters, but it's how I use my gifts and talents to serve others. The meticulous janitor, the person with the earned G.E.D., and the vocational school graduate, are worthy of the same respect as the hard working doctor, the high school graduate, and the Harvard alumni.

One

Jane's Child

God's greatest commandment begins with, *"Love your neighbor as yourself."* This great command begs the question: How do we love others, if we don't love ourselves? How do we love ourselves in our darkest moments?

My great-great-grandmother, Jane, was born a slave. She was stripped of her surname, her parents, and her freedom. She was raped. She didn't know her date of birth. She was robbed of the right to a formal education. She was illiterate. Yet, she was a rock. A rock whose love for her children never wavered. Thus, she gave birth to the most influential and powerful Black leader of his time, my great-grandfather, Booker T. Washington.

To me and probably to my great-grandfather, Booker T. Washington, his mother and my great-great-grandmother, Jane, would always remain the noblest embodiment of womanhood. Jane never had a book of her own but was a strict teacher and observer. Jane was a mastermind who demonstrated skills of integrity, and leading a sensible and practical life.

No matter what the circumstance, Jane was determined to instill the best values possible in her children. She was a strong woman with an iron will. During a time when slave women were forced to comply with sexual advances by their masters on a regular basis, Jane gave birth to my great-grandfather Booker Taliaferro, his brother John, and his sister Amanda. Although rumor had it that Booker was fathered by a White neighbor, I would imagine that my great-great grandmother's master was not an innocent bystander.

My great-great-grandmother had to bravely raise her three slave children when there was nothing to look forward to other than daily degradation. She endured humiliation, hard-labor, poverty, pain and suffering. Booker Taliaferro was born on the Burroughs Plantation, near Hale's Ford, in Franklin County, Virginia.

My great-great-grandmother, Jane, was the plantation cook. She and her three children lived in a small one room log cabin about 12 x 16 feet, without any windows. The cabin also served as the kitchen. They all slept on the dirt floor of the cabin and dedicated the remaining space to the Burroughs family's nutritional needs. In the center of the floor there was an opening where sweet potatoes were kept for the master's family. Her days were long and tedious, starting at sunrise and ending late into the night. She was responsible for everything related to the meal, including slaughtering the meat, gathering sticks from the woods, and making the fire on which to cook. All of the cooking was done in pots and skillets over an open fireplace, located in the cabin. Jane and her children remained in that cabin until freedom came when my great-grandfather, Booker T. Washington, was 9-years-old.

Jane married a slave named Washington, who lived on another plantation and belonged to the Ferguson family. "Wash" as they called him, fled to West Virginia during the Civil War; and after

Emancipation, Jane moved her family to West Virginia to rejoin her husband.

Despite all of her slave responsibilities, my great-great grandmother had very little time to give attention to the training of her children. Still, somehow Jane managed to snatch a few moments for their emotional and spiritual care, either early in the morning or late at night. She would always encourage young Booker to maintain his dream about going to a schoolhouse where he could study like the White boys and girls that he was in servitude to. Jane kept herself informed through the "grape-vine" telegraph and was inspired by learning that freedom was in the near future. It became a daily ritual for Jane to involve her children as they prayed fervently to be delivered up from slavery.

Upon freedom, Booker's mother gathered her three children and they made the long journey to West Virginia to be with her husband. During the trip Jane would build fires to cook their meals, and build pallets for them to sleep on. They walked the greater portion of the several hundred mile trip, which took several weeks to complete. Had my great-great-grandmother given up or given in, it's quite possible that I wouldn't be here today. This is true for so many African-Americans. *If not for the tenacity of our ancestors, where would any of us be?*

When they settled in West Virginia, Booker persuaded his mother to get a "blue-back" spelling book for him so that he could teach himself to read. *Noah Webster's blue-backed speller books taught five generations of American children how to spell and read.* In his auto-biography Booker explained that he didn't know how his mother got the book, but she did. He wrote, "In all my efforts to learn to read, my mother shared full my ambition, and sympathized with me, and aided me in every way that she could. Though she was totally ignorant, so far as mere book knowledge was concerned, she had high ambitions for her children, and a large fund of good hard, common sense which seemed to enable her to meet and master every situation. If I have done anything in life worth attention, I feel sure that I inherited the disposition from my mother."

Had Jane not encouraged Booker to follow his dream of getting an education, and instead bought into the nonsense that we were not "fully human," he may have taken a very different path—one of self-destruction, instead of self-determination. In which case, there would be no Tuskegee University, and more importantly, the thousands upon thousands of great minds that have come out of Tuskegee may have taken different paths as well, instead of coming back into our communities as role models and leaders for the next generation.

Somehow, the spirit, encouragement, and prayers of my great-great-grandmother Jane must have seeped down to me; as I, like my great-grandfather Booker, and my mother, developed a fervent love for reading and writing, and a thirst for education. Writing was especially a constant in the back of my mind. Even when my teen years became tumultuous and difficult to endure, writing was my most powerful outlet.

To her oppressors, my great-great-grandmother was worth nothing; but to me—she was worth everything. She was a queen, and my maternal family's first known matriarch. Jane laid a firm foundation, and it was up to us to continue building upon it. *But would we?*

Success Principle One — Don't Give Up, Don't Give In

How were our ancestors able to do so much more with so much less? They did not have anywhere near the resources we have on our hands today. They made it through much harsher trials than we can even imagine. And they did this with no cell phones, no computers, no email, Facebook, or Twitter, and no formal education. Without a doubt, the reason the majority of African-Americans are able to enjoy these privileges now is because our ancestors were determined not to give up, and they refused to give in.

My great-grandfather once said, "Let us keep before us the fact that, almost without exception, every race or nation that has ever got upon its feet has done so through struggle and trial and persecution; and that out of this very resistance to wrong, out of the struggle against odds, they have gained strength, self-confidence, and experience which they could not have gained in any other way."

In other words, trials are here to teach us something. Don't run from them, because if you run you will only tire yourself out. Don't sweep them under the rug, because if you sweep them under the rug, they will always be in your midst, lingering— seeping out, little by little.

Success Tips

❖ Prepare for trials before they come by always developing yourself emotionally, spiritually, and intellectually.

❖ Use the same strengths that got you through prior trials, to get through present trials.

❖ Be open to searching for the lesson, which is the silver-lining in every trial you face.

"Years ago I resolved that because I had no ancestry myself I would leave a record of which my children would be proud, and which might encourage them to still higher effort."

—Booker T. Washington

What I've Learned from my Great-Grandfather's life

There are two ways that I can view any situation. One is hopeful, the other is doubtful. If I choose hope, I am more likely to find something positive in each situation. If I choose doubt, I am likely to breed negativity into the existing circumstance.

Two
Blue Blood or Accident of Birth

Outside of his mother, Booker T. Washington had no known ancestry, so he was determined to leave a record, which his children and their descendants would be proud of, and which might encourage them to strive higher.

Apparently, my mother (his granddaughter), Agnes Louise Washington, didn't receive that memo. Her plans didn't line up with my great-grandfather's plan at all. They didn't even come close.

Momma never talked about her grandfather, Booker T. Washington… it was as if he didn't exist…let alone being a part of our direct lineage. I was the last born of his great-grandchildren. Yet, I didn't understand the significance of what that meant, or the significance of who he was—a former slave turned famous educator, and founder of Tuskegee Institute, today known as Tuskegee University.

My mother didn't talk much about her childhood either. She was the oldest of four girls, born to Booker T. Washington's youngest child, Ernest Davidson Washington. Momma was born in 1919, four years after Booker T. Washington died in 1915. I heard that my mother and her sisters, Margaret Washington Clifford, Edith Washington Johnson, and Gloria Washington Jackson, had a sort of "royal" existence growing up as the granddaughters of Booker T. Washington. They were born and raised in a home across from Tuskegee University…a home that Booker T Washington, had given to their parents as a wedding gift. They had a pleasant upbringing, with affable surroundings, and good parenting. They didn't have lots of money, but as Booker T. Washington's granddaughters, they had his noble blood running through their veins. The whole town knew that. They bore the Washington name and that name came with prestige. It was a name held in high esteem, a name of honor and respect…an extraordinary family legacy that money could not buy.

Although Booker T. Washington died four years prior to my mother's birth, as a result of her upbringing and lineage, she and her three sisters lived their entire childhood in the midst of his greatness. She had great and monumental experiences throughout her childhood and young adult life; and was surrounded by famous and influential people who highly respected Booker T. Washington. My Aunt Edith's godfather was the famous scientist, George Washington Carver. Carver came to Tuskegee in 1896 upon Booker T. Washington's invitation to head up Tuskegee's agricultural department.

However, Momma was very modest and low key. By the time my brother James and I came along, which was much later in her life, she had played down her prestigious lineage. Even though my mother grew up surrounded by so many positive influences, until her passing in 1999, many of her close acquaintances never knew anything about her lineage.

As an adult, I have learned that from its earliest existence, Tuskegee Institute was a family affair of able-bodied sisters, brothers, aunts and uncles who worked there—made up of mostly former slaves and their descendants. This reality was further realized one Sunday afternoon as I watched Lionel Ritchie on "Oprah's Master Class." Ritchie (whose grandmother, Mrs. Foster, lived next door to my grandparents, my mother, and her sisters) explained how he was born on the campus of Tuskegee Institute. He referred to Tuskegee as "the bubble." He said what went on inside of the bubble and what went on outside of the bubble were two different worlds. He said that outside of the bubble was the Klan and segregation. As a picture of the Tuskegee Airmen flashed across the screen, he described the inside of the bubble as a place where some of the greatest minds in America—doctors, lawyers, engineers, professors, and pilots—resided.

Ritchie went on to refer to Black colleges as the Mecca for mental power, because back then, as he put it, "There was no place else for them to go." He said while there was nothing unusual about seeing Black doctors and lawyers in Tuskegee, in the nearby town of Montgomery, Blacks were neither allowed to vote nor to drink from the same water fountains as Whites. That was enlightening for me—to learn that Tuskegee had been a wall of protection for Blacks. Now, in the 21st century, I wonder why there are not more walls of protection in the communities where Black on Black murder rates skyrocket across America.

When my Aunt Margaret died in 2009, Lionel Ritchie had a beautiful bouquet of white flowers delivered to her gravesite on the campus of Tuskegee University. She is buried there amidst many other prominent African-Americans, including Booker T. Washington, George Washington Carver, and my great-grand-mother, Olivia Davidson Washington.

Olivia Davidson was a primary fundraiser, a teacher, and a co-founder of Tuskegee Institute. Three days after she gave birth to my mother's father, on February 6, 1889, their house burned down and she suffered exposure to the early morning cold. Never fully recovering, she died three months later, on May 9th 1889, when she succumbed to laryngeal tuberculosis. At the time, my grandfather,

Ernest Davidson, had an older brother Booker, Jr. and a step-sister Portia, who was Booker T. Washington's first-born child.

Momma was very close to her father. When he died she was devastated. She was 19-years-old at that time, and away at Tennessee State University. When she received the news she rushed home to Tuskegee to be with her mother and her sisters. It's possible that her adoring father dying when she was just 19-years-old could have contributed to her detached concept of who she was. Whatever it was, it was an insecure trait that she would inevitably pass down to me.

Like Booker T. Washington, Momma believed you had to earn everything through hard work, and nothing should ever be handed to you. And that's okay...but our lineage...why couldn't we have that? *When you don't know where you started from, you're bound to get lost.*

Often I wonder how our lives may have been different if, when we were children misbehaving, we were reminded by our parents, "You are a Washington—Washingtons don't behave that way." To the contrary, when I would bring up our lineage, Momma would simply and kindly say, "It was merely an accident of birth." And that was the end of the conversation. What kind of childhood might I have experienced, having the knowledge that I was a direct descendant of such a great man; and having his values, integrity and spiritual beliefs passed on to me through stories my mother could have told me about his life, and her upbringing?

Perhaps when I was growing up in the infamous "Sixties" in North Oakland, California, Momma didn't talk about her heritage because a Black revolution was on the rise. The most militant part of this unrest started right in our North Oakland neighborhood, literally almost in our backyard, when Huey P. Newton, along with Bobby Seale, organized the Black Panther Party. It was 1966 and I was 7-years-old. It was the dawn of the assassinations of John F. Kennedy, Medgar Evers, and Malcolm X—on the heels of the riots in Watts, California—and at the peak of the civil rights movement led by Martin Luther King, Jr. Understandably, Blacks were growing weary of the injustices and oppression that continued to plague them. At that time, it was common for infuriated Blacks to label, the then deceased, Booker T. Washington an "Uncle Tom," because of his non-confrontational philosophy.

Or, it may have been that my mother could no longer embrace her lineage because she believed that the only reason my father married her was because she was a Washington. Whatever the reason was for her silence, it left a huge void in my life.

Many years would pass before I began to realize that I was not an accident of birth because God doesn't make mistakes. To the contrary, He creates miracles, and in our favor and privilege He places us strategically and exclusively to be used to fulfill a higher purpose. Eventually I would take in the fact that I had the blood of a great man running through my veins. And after many dangers, toils, and snares, I'd find that out.

Success Principle Two — Connecting the Past to Inspire the Future

When I was growing up the writers of our textbooks didn't elaborate on my great-grandfather's work, or the work of many other of our great ancestors. There was a blurb in our school books about Tuskegee Institute; but nothing of the magnitude of how Booker T. Washington, and his cohorts, improved the lives of the masses of former slaves and their descendants in America.

In the South, many schools have required students to read "Up From Slavery." They were also required to read about Frederick Douglass, W.E.B. Dubois, and other African-American leaders.

This gave them a richer and a much broader perspective on the significant role Blacks played in improving the moral conscientiousness of the nation, and in developing the landscape throughout the United States. This is quite possibly one of the reasons that there is a distinct difference in the attitudes, behaviors, and the culture of African-Americans from the South.

Success Tips

❖ Visit libraries, museums, and bookstores to improve your knowledge about your history, and pass that knowledge along to at least one child.

❖ Never forget where you come from, no matter how far your journey has taken you, because someone else needs to know how to get to where you are.

❖ Our past should not make us bitter, it should make us better. It should not make us angry, it should make us realize just how remarkable we are. From here we will continue to rise.

Special Memories from the Booker T. Washington Family Photo Collection

Great-Grandmother,
Olivia Davidson Washington
(6/11/1854-5/8/1889)
A Co-Founder of Tuskegee Institute

Sarah Meriwether Nutter, Great Aunt,
Namesake,
A Co-founder of AKA Sorority
(1/1/1888—4/10/1950)

Reconstruction of Booker T. Washington's childhood cabin
(a national historic site) on the plantation, located in Franklin County, Virginia

Tuskegee Normal & Industrial Institute (1881)

Booker T. Washington, Booker T. Washington, II
and Ernest Davidson Washington (Sarah's Grandfather)

Booker T. Washington and his two Sons Booker T. Washington II (center) and
Ernest Davidson Washington (right) on Horseback

Family-Sisters, Aunt Margaret (top) & Agnes Louise (Sarah's Mother)

The four daughters of Ernest Davidson Washington –
Margaret, Gloria, Agnes Louise, (right to left) and Edith (standing)
in front of the Lifting The Veil Statue at Tuskegee University

Gloria, Agnes Louise, Margaret, Edith

Tuskegee Airmen (1942) with Uncle Cab (Marshall Cabiness), 2nd to Left

Sarah's parents - Agnes Louise Washington O'Neal and James Lyle O'Neal

"There are two ways of exerting one's strength; one is by pushing down, the other is by pulling up."

—Booker T. Washington

What I've Learned from my Great-Grandfather's life

I must understand that no one, including myself, is perfect. I must not attempt to change others to fit into how I think they should be, but rather, I should encourage them to be their best, and I should meet them where they are.

Three
Fall From Grace

When I was born, my parents, Agnes Louise Washington and James Lyle O'Neal, had been married to each other for the second time around. If their first marriage was rocky, the second one was tumultuous. At best, my parents had a love-hate relationship. From as early as I can remember, Momma and Daddy were constantly at each other's throats, yelling and screaming, and attacking one another's characters. I believe they were unconsciously trying to destroy each other's self-worth—at which I am convinced they succeeded. By the time their second marriage ended, the hate appeared to far outweigh whatever love was left.

When my brother James and I were born, my parents were older... and on their second go round with children. When I was born my father was 45, and my mother was almost 40. I don't believe they were trying to add to their family, considering they were not the happiest of married couples, and there were quite a number of years between us and their older children. At the time, birth control wasn't around, and abortions were illegal. *I've often wondered if I would be here if that wasn't the case.* If it were up to my parents, I somehow doubt it, but thankfully God had other plans.

My parents first met aboard the first USS Liberty Ship to be named after a famous African-American, my mother's grandfather, Booker T Washington. It was customary for the female direct descendants of such an influential man to be accompanied by a male escort. Right around the time the ship was to be dedicated, my father was named by his fraternity, Kappa Alpha Psi, "the most eligible bachelor in Los Angeles." Thus, he was selected as the most suitable man to escort my mother for this most honorable occasion.

When they met, it seemed to be a perfect union, a match made in heaven; but only time would tell. I suspect they were excited initially, but my mother would later accuse my father of many faults, the most significant being that he only married her because of her famous family lineage. This bitter disenchantment may have also contributed to why my mother later kept quiet about her grandfather's legacy.

For many years of her life, Momma was a diamond in the rough. Though I am not sure if she ever realized it, Momma was very pretty. Like her mother and her three sisters, she was the epitome of the term, "lady-like." Her beautiful wavy shoulder length black hair was a nice contrast to her deep brown eyes. Momma was very dainty. Small in stature, she stood about 5'3". She had very fair skin, and looked more White than Black. But you couldn't tell her that. She was proud to be a Black woman and would become very upset if she was mistaken for White. Living through the discrimination in the South in the early 1900's, Momma could have easily passed, but she never would. She was committed and proud to be with her people in the struggle. Truth-telling, and being proud to be Black, were two of the better qualities she passed on to me.

My mother was a member of the nation's oldest Black sorority, Alpha Kappa Alpha (AKA). Her maternal aunt, my namesake, Sarah Meriwether Nutter, was one of the founders of AKA at

Howard University in Washington, D.C., in 1908. She was my grandmother's sister. Momma said when I was born my grandmother wanted to name me Mary Louise, but Momma overruled her mother, and named me after her favorite Aunt Sarah, because she didn't have children of her own.

Before Momma and Daddy met, Momma was making quite an exciting life for herself. Like her grandfather, she was a workaholic at heart. It wasn't until she was interviewed much later in her life that I learned of several of the honorable positions she held as a young woman. In Tuskegee she worked at the Tuskegee air base for the Tuskegee Airmen by day...and she partied with them at night. Her sister, Margaret, married one of the pilots, Marshall Cabiness. After graduating from college, Momma moved to Washington, D.C., where she worked for Howard Thurman during the day, and Mary McLeod Bethune in the evening; and where she was the first African-American to work in the Department of Agriculture. On her way to the dedication of the USS Liberty ship to be named after Booker T. Washington, Momma traveled by train with Marian Anderson, who was performing at the prestigious event...the event where my parents met.

Momma was book smart and she excelled at anything she put her mind to, especially academics. At the age of 17 she left home in Tuskegee, Alabama to attend Tennessee State University. Three years later, at the age of 20, she received her bachelor's degree in Office Management, one of the few fields open to women at that time. She was a passionate reader. She loved and cherished books. Sometimes she'd be reading three books at the same time...one for just before bedtime, one for unwinding after work, and one for the restroom. Momma once told me that reading was her escape. She was fascinated by the characters she read about and said that when she reads it's as if she is living vicariously through them. Thus, she never read anything scary or sad. She only read romantic novels and inspirational books, like biographies of those she admired.

Most likely, she would be absorbed in a Danielle Steel or Harlequin Romance novel, or a biography of someone she thought highly of, such as: Dorothy Dandridge, Jacqueline Kennedy, Lady Bird Johnson, Coretta Scott King, or Princess Diana. Had she lived to see this side of history, I am certain that Momma would have already read any and every book written about President Barack and Michelle Obama…as long as it was positive.

Early on, Momma ingrained in me the idea that books were to be treasured and handled with the utmost of care. I still get inspired by the memories I get when I go into a bookstore or library. Momma always bought Dr. Seuss books for us: I particularly remember: "Cat in the Hat", "Green Eggs and Ham" and "Are You My Mother?" She also made sure there was always a dictionary and an updated set of encyclopedias in the house. Whenever I would ask her a question about something, she made me look it up. To this day, unless I am in a hurry, before I ask a question I first try to find the answer on my own. When I was a little girl, like so many other little girls, I felt that my mother was the smartest person on earth.

My father was very handsome. His brown caramel color skin tone complimented his pretty hazel eyes, which I inherited in a slightly darker version from him. Much taller than my mother, he stood about 6'2"; and he had a very strong physique. He was a Master Mason and a member of the Kappa Alpha Psi fraternity. After earning his undergraduate degree from UCLA in international relations, he went on to earn a law degree from Texas Southern University in 1938. While at UCLA he was a Pacific Coast Inter-collegiate boxing champion, football player, and a track star. Daddy often boasted of being dubbed "Big Man on Campus" at UCLA. He undoubtedly inherited his athletic ability and career ambitions from his uncle, all-time football great, Duke Slater, who played football at the University of Iowa from 1918 to 1921.

Although Slater helped to lead Iowa to an undefeated season in 1921, he never finished higher than second team All-American. Only later was the injustice corrected. Duke Slater is noted as one of two Iowa players who was elected to the College Football Hall of Fame in its inaugural year of 1951. He played ten years of professional football with the American Football League and then signed a contract with the Chicago Cardinals of the National Football League, becoming one of five black players in the league. Duke was the first African-American lineman in NFL history, and one of the most outstanding linemen of his era.

At least once or twice, my mother told me about my father's eye for her first cousin, Nettie Washington Douglass. Momma said Daddy settled for her because his first choice, Nettie, was spoken for, and would not have him. She was glamorous. There's no doubt Nettie was quite a woman. From the pictures I've seen of her, she was strikingly beautiful, with a radiant smile, and abounding confidence. Nettie was the daughter of Booker T. Washington's second child, Booker T. Washington, Jr.

Nettie married Frederick Douglass's grandson, making their offspring direct descendants of two very famous Black men. My mother described her as a "show stopper." She said that when Nettie would enter a room all eyes were on her. People would stop in midsentence to take notice. She only had one thing that my mother didn't have, and that was a high level of self-assurance. Although my mother accused my father of desiring Nettie, Momma always spoke highly of her. I never heard her say a cross word about her beautiful cousin. In spite of everything that went on in her personal life, whether my mother recognized it or not, she remained a very classy lady…that was something ingrained in her upbringing, and something she could not shake, even if she wanted to.

From the stories I've heard, there's also little doubt that Nettie was the only woman my father had eyes for. My grandmother never wanted my mother to marry my father. According to my mother, her mother had reservations from the very beginning. By all accounts, my grandmother was very wise, and her gut instinct told her my father was not ready to settle down and make a comfortable life for her eldest daughter.

When I was a young adult, Momma often repeated one of her mother's cliché's, "It's as easy to fall in love with a rich man as it is to fall in love with a poor man." That was her sound advice. Two of my aunts married physicians. My other aunt married one of the Tuskegee Airmen. My mother met and married my father who graduated from law school, but never fulfilled his dream of becoming an attorney. Facetiously Momma would say, "He never passed *the Bar* because he could never pass *a bar*." But my father contended that it was because of the discrimination he faced when he graduated from law school in Texas in 1938. Both stories may have a ring of truth to them. However, in the long run, whatever it was, I am convinced it created a sense of failure and bitterness that my father carried for most of his life.

Despite the discrimination that festered throughout the country my father's uncle, Duke Slater earned a law degree from Iowa, and passed the bar. Slater later moved to Chicago and became an assistant district attorney. In 1948, he became the second African-American elected as a judge in Chicago when he won election to the city's Municipal Court. In 1960 Slater became the first Black member of the Chicago Superior Court, then the highest court in the city. He moved to the Circuit Court of Cook County in 1964, following that institution's formation. Undoubtedly, my father's failure to follow in his uncle's footsteps and to fulfill his dream interfered with his ability to love and cherish my mother, and to provide a decent quality of life for his children.

One day, when my father was in his late seventies, clad in his lounging clothes and slippers, he boarded a Greyhound bus to confront the issue he'd been haunted by for over forty years. He was older than his years because he drank most of his life away. Nevertheless, he went to Texas Southern University to demand an apology. Upon receiving a written apology, he got back on a bus and returned to Los Angeles. I'm not sure of the authenticity of the letter, but it gave him the sense of satisfaction that he longed for.

Memories of my parents ever living together are vague at best. I have a blurred memory from when I was four, living in the upstairs unit of a white stucco two-story home in Berkeley. I remember that because Daddy later moved up the street from there when I was a little older, which helped to seal whatever pleasant childhood memories I managed to hold onto. Daddy often boasted that the great jazz vibraphonist, pianist, percussionist, bandleader and actor, Lionel Hampton, visited us when we lived there. Downstairs was some sort of small business, possibly an insurance or tax office. As young as I was, I have an obscure recollection of tension and bickering between my parents.

My earliest vivid memories occurred when I was around 5-years-old. Momma, James, and I lived on 61st and Grove Street in North Oakland. We lived two doors down from, and went to school with Rickey Henderson. Little did I know, my friend and neighbor would grow up to be named the American League's Most Valuable Player in 1990, become the leadoff hitter for two World Series Championships: the 1989 Oakland A's and the 1993 Toronto Blue Jays, and be inducted into the Baseball Hall of Fame as one of the greatest players to ever play the game. One thing I admire about Rickey and his wife, Pamela, is that they are more down-to-earth than other people I am acquainted with who have far less accomplishments.

We lived in a decent, low to median income, working class neighborhood. Momma was a single parent by then. We lived there until I was 12-years-old. My father lived across the street and several houses down from us in North Oakland. Daddy always managed to live in close proximity to us in our younger years, which my brother and I were overjoyed by, and my mother was highly annoyed and agitated by.

Because Daddy lived so close, he was often aware of our visitors. One particular morning when my mother was in the back room on the pullout sofa bed with her boyfriend, my father came busting through the back door yelling at the top of his lungs, "What are you doing in bed with this man? You have children in here!" Had it not been for his screaming and waking us up, we wouldn't have known about it because we were tucked in our beds in the front room.

Daddy was a big man, and I am certain Momma's boyfriend was uneasy, at the very least, because he was quite a bit smaller in stature. Not to mention he was probably more embarrassed than afraid as he laid there. I don't remember how it ended, but I suspect the boyfriend got dressed and ran out. As young as I was, I believe Daddy was more jealous than concerned about us. Besides, compared to what he did with women when we were in his care, he made Momma look like a saint. No doubt, this is why today I have no tolerance for parents who use their kids to hurt or manipulate each other. It's also undoubtedly the reason I would end up in one unhealthy relationship after another, well into my adult years.

Shortly after Daddy's big scene with Momma, I can remember one day pleading with Momma to let me visit with my friend, Derek, two doors down. We were both in kindergarten. I considered him my boyfriend…at least one day I did. His mom made the fluffiest pancakes I'd ever seen. They tasted as fabulous as they looked. I remember eating pancakes with Derek and his mom a number of times, although I'm not sure why I was at his house eating breakfast so often, at 5-years-old. On this particular day, after Momma finally said I could go play with him, we were caught hugging under the playground equipment in his backyard. I am not sure what we called ourselves doing, but we were fully clothed, and I got in some sort of trouble. I was probably imitating something I'd seen her or my father doing. In my professional training, *I have learned that from infancy to around 12-years-old children learn the most by watching others.*

My parents had countless arguments about child support that my dad didn't pay. My mother would always threaten to put him in jail. The verbal abuse that I witnessed between them took place during some of the most formative years of my childhood, when my personality was forming and my brain was developing. I don't remember their actual words; I probably unconsciously blocked them out in an effort to protect myself. However, I can't help but believe those words seeped into my subconscious and helped shape who I would become. I suspect the nine months leading to my birth were no picnic for me either. This type of child-rearing behavior breeds life into the saying, "It's easier to build up a child, than it is to repair an adult."

There are only two things that I can ever remember my parents agreeing on. The first was that my mother had an extremely strong work ethic and was brilliant at any task she took on. But that was not a secret. Even those who only slightly knew her, knew that about her. When we had a devastating earthquake in 1989, two weeks short of Momma's seventieth birthday, I was so worried about her. The phones were off, the lights were out, freeways had collapsed, fires were started, gas stations were closed, and my car was on empty. When I was finally able to get to her, several hours later, I found Momma with a flashlight in her hand, working diligently to ensure that all of her residents were safe.

The second area they agreed on, was that education was of primary importance. They were both college graduates, who had been raised by parents with the legacy of Booker T. Washington constantly on their minds. Because these two values were ingrained in me at an early age, by both my parents, I have excelled in both areas—work ethics and education. This demonstrates the power of parental agreement in the mind of a child. And it works both ways— productively and destructively.

We always had a cat. Momma loved cats, and she sometimes seemed to love our cats more than she loved most people. It was probably because they didn't talk back, required very low maintenance, and basically took care of themselves. The two cats I remember most were, a jet black tabby named Huey, after the founder of the Black Panther Party, and Diana. Diana gave birth to a couple of litters in our clothes closet. It was somewhat fascinating to watch how much pleasure it gave Momma to take care of the kittens until they were old enough to give away.

Momma would have had a fit if she knew that sometimes James and I would drop Huey and Diana, and sometimes the older kittens, down from the top of the staircase to prove over and over that they would land on their feet. Unlike so many others in our life, they never let us down. In case it was true that cats only had nine lives, we kept count of how many times they'd been dropped, and we never did it a tenth time…as if somehow that made us sensitive.

During the week Momma's boyfriend would come over, the same one my father kicked out the bed, and the only boyfriend I have ever known Momma to have. I once overheard Momma speaking to a girlfriend about the fact that her boyfriend was married. They would listen to jazz all evening. They were both jazz lovers. He would sometimes bring over his big bass, sit it upright on the floor, and play to the music on the stereo. Once in a while he'd take Momma out to dinner and to listen to live jazz. Because he was married, I am not sure how he was able to pull that off, but he did. He was pleasant and nice to my brother and me. Once I playfully referred to him as "daddy" and I got the most humiliating scolding of my life from Momma. Needless to say, I never did that again.

To this day, because of that scolding, I am careful how I address people. He really seemed to be into Momma. I never heard them argue or fight. Now, as I think back, I believe Momma was just containing her real feelings, settling because she didn't think she deserved a man all to herself. The story was that he stayed married only because he and his wife were Catholic and Catholics didn't believe in divorce. But adultery was okay? Really?!

About the time Momma entered her early fifties, she finally got fed up with the relationship, and most likely the disgraceful lifestyle; so she stopped seeing him and answering his calls. Once she was done, she was done. After that, she gave up on men, and for the last 25 years of her life, she never got into another intimate relationship again, which didn't seem to bother her at all. For all of those years she would receive hang up calls, which she believed were from him. As far as I know, he never got divorced. Momma would later replace men with more work, more books, and travel, which included taking trips to her favorite place on earth, Europe.

I admire Momma for walking away from that relationship, and for channeling her energy in positive directions. I only wish that some of that energy would have been channeled toward embracing our rich heritage. Instead, it's as if she put it on a shelf, and walked away from that as well. Thus, by the time I was born, there was very little evidence that my life had any real meaning, and perhaps, as my mother would often tell me, "it was just an accident of birth." Although my lineage was rich, considered by many to be blueblood, my upbringing was not.

Success Principle Three— Perspective is Everything

As the great philosopher, Henry David Thoreau, so accurately stated, "It's not what you look at that matters, it's what you see."

While helping to organize a mental health workshop at my church, I was given a meditation to pass out to all the attendees. In part, the meditation read: *The human mind is so delicate and so complex that only its Maker can know it wholly. Each mind is so different, actuated by such different motives, controlled by such different circumstances, influenced by such different sufferings; you cannot know all the influences that have gone to make up a personality.*

This meditation beautifully explains why no two people see the world the same. The combinations of life events behind the way individuals see things are often unconscious. Some people believe that perspective begins to develop in the womb. That's why expecting mothers sometimes read, talk, and sing to their unborn baby.

For certain, perspective begins to form once a baby is born. In the womb they are automatically fed, and they are not uncomfortable by soiled diapers. Once they are born they often are in a measure of distress until they are fed and/ or have their diapers changed. As you can imagine, the length of time, and the frequency of positive or negative experiences in getting these primary needs met, is going to have an impact on their perspectives about whether life is good or whether life is bad.

Success Tips

❖ When a situation causes a significant amount of emotional difficulty, deliberately changing your perspective from negative to positive may be all that is needed to change how you feel. Dwelling on the negative only contributes to its power.

❖ Never judge someone, or be too hard on yourself, for seeking counseling because often that is the most effective way to bring awareness to how negative perspectives developed, so that you can change them.

❖ Taking in, and reciting the above meditation, may create peace, by turning irritation to compassion toward those who may behave in ways that are difficult to tolerate.

"There are too many people in the world who give their whole lives grasping at the shadow instead of the substance."

–Booker T. Washington

What I've Learned from my Great-Grandfather's life

In order to get the most out of life, it's important that I look beyond the surface. While it is nice and sometimes more comforting to have material gain, when I look more deeply into my spiritual and humanistic values and principles, my life becomes more meaningful.

Four

Daddy's Girl

Unlike my mother, Daddy took great pride in the fact that we were direct descendants of Booker T. Washington…which was just another bone of contention for Momma. I'm not sure if he ever introduced my brother and me as James and Sarah when we were children. Instead, Daddy would always start the introduction with what seemed to be as much strength as he could muster up, "These are the great-grandchildren of Booker T Washington!" We would cringe with embarrassment, partly because we didn't understand why he was so excited, partly because most people didn't believe him, and partly because my mother raised us with an extremely different take. Had Daddy sat me down and taught me what the textbooks would not, I may have been just as excited and as proud as he was.

On one occasion, when I was 9-years-old, my father took my brother and me for a walk around the neighborhood, as he often did. As we approached an elderly man on the street…I don't even think my father knew him, but that wasn't a requirement…Daddy made his usual introduction. The man looked down at me and apparently noticed my embarrassment more than my brother's, because he looked directly in my eyes and said, "Don't be ashamed, that is a great privilege and I am honored to meet a descendant of such a great man and to know his descendants are among us." His comment stuck with me, but it didn't stick with me as strongly as my mother's words and attitude about our lineage.

My parent's turbulent relationship included twists and turns which produced five children. Before Momma and Daddy met, my father had a daughter, my late sister Lynne. Lynne sadly lost her battle to cancer in 2011. She was 18 years older than me. When I first met her, she was in her forties. Lynne was very kind, and she was always supportive, interested, and excited about my work with troubled youth. She was a public school teacher in Los Angeles for many years. Our father's facial features were dominant in both of us, and we looked a lot alike. Two weeks before she died I went to Los Angeles to visit her. We went to lunch and talked for hours. One thing she told me that was somewhat shocking to me, was that my father didn't form a relationship with her until she was in her twenties. She wasn't bitter or complaining, just stating a fact.

Momma and Daddy got married the first time when Lynne was 3-years-old. During their first marriage, my sister Edith, who is 15 years my senior, was born. When my parents divorced the first time, my sister Edith had to be around 2-years-old, because my mother married someone else, and she and her new husband had my estranged brother, Johnny, who is 13 years my senior.

Several years following my mother's divorce to Johnny's father, she got back together with my father. They remarried for the second time. During this marriage, my brother James was born, and then two years later, I was born. By the time I was 5-years-old, my parents were divorced again.

When I was three-years-old, my sister Edith left our home in Oakland to attend our great-grandfather's school, Tuskegee University. Once Edith left, she never came back. Momma and Daddy's constant arguing likely contributed to her leaving and to her decision not to return to California. I was too young to remember her ever living with us. I remember her giving me sound advice when I was in a terrible relationship. She said, "When you are ready to leave, you will leave with only the clothes on your back." In other words, stop with all the excuses for why you are staying. Edith married an attorney in Flint, Michigan, and they had three children before he died unexpectedly from a heart attack.

Needless to say, I wouldn't hear any great stories about my father from my mother. But I would hear them from one of Daddy's favorite nieces, former United States Congresswoman, Diane Watson. Her late mother, Aunt Dorothy, and my father were brother and sister. Cousin Diane is very passionate about family, and she has always been the most wonderful narrator of our family history on my father's side—even in the midst of her work in Congress and beyond.

The stories Cousin Diane told, and still tells, occurred well before I was ever thought of. Because my parents were up in age when I was born, I am the youngest of my first cousins on both sides of my family. I didn't have many of the same family experiences as they had. Cousin Diane was very close to my father when she was growing up, and she helps me to see a broader view of who he truly was.

Her stories about Daddy are fascinating. They included many interesting facets of his life, such as: his years as a champion athlete at UCLA; his relationship with the former mayor of Los Angeles, Tom

Bradley, whom he met when they were attending UCLA together; his work as a Los Angeles police officer, as well as his philosophical views. Whenever Diane describes her "Uncle James," her face lights up, and she uses the word "brilliant", without fail. When Daddy passed away in 1996 she arranged a memorial service that was fit for a king. Diane was very fond of Daddy, and Daddy was extremely proud of his niece. If not for her, I might have a pretty one-sided view of my father.

I did know that Daddy was a self-proclaimed philosopher. He would often say, in his most scholarly, deep voice, "This too shall pass," or "Whatever will be, will be." I will also never forget the lesson he taught me when a handicapped child was passing by us. He said, "Don't ever laugh at anyone who has a disability. Instead, thank God that you are free from any physical limitations." I didn't realize then, but I know now that those were just seeds that Daddy was dropping into our life, that God would later water.

From as early as around 5-years-old, I remember there was this song he'd often sing. In his most deep and serious tone of voice, as if he were singing classical opera, he began the song, "Gee, but I'd give the world to see that old gang of mine..." Every time he'd start crooning, "Geeee," James and I would interrupt, and bellow out, "whiz." Then we'd bust out laughing as my father went on to finish the song, as he tried to stay serious, but he was always unable to hold back a laugh. I can't count the number of times we repeated this routine. If we did this once, we did it a thousand times.

I was deemed, appropriately by my mother, "daddy's girl." She would often say in a very cynical and facetious tone, laced with a hint of jealousy, "You are your father's child...in your eyes he can't do anything wrong." She was right. I adored my Daddy. Though my perspective would change as an adult, when I was a child my father was, without a doubt, my favorite parent.

Momma was tasked with the important work, including, checking our homework, taking us to doctors and dentist appointments, and disciplining us. So it's no wonder that she was our least favorite parent. When she came home in the evening she fed us stuff we didn't want to eat, helped us with homework, gave us baths, and made sure we were in bed on time. In the midst of all of that, she paid the bills and, from time to time, met with our teachers. It was Momma who took care of us and handled all of the necessary tasks that would assure us of having a healthy and stable environment. As children, however, we didn't realize that she was the one who made sure we survived in the best way she knew how. All Daddy did was make sure we were happy and having fun.

From Monday through Friday Daddy worked hard as a special representative of the Pacific Division of Falstaff Brewery Company for northern California and northern Nevada. Daddy was a great salesman, the first African-American to represent his territory in the Bay Area, which included a part of West Oakland where all the other salesmen were afraid to go. They gave him a brand new car every other year, right off the showroom floor. He always let me and James go with him, and would always let us pick out the car. The one most vivid in my memory was a long emerald green Chevrolet Impala.

Every week, with great anticipation, I waited for Friday to come because with the rare exception when he was on a business trip, after my father got off work, he would always pick us up and take us to his place to spend the entire weekend. To our delight, when we went to his house there was no order, and there was no structure. While we considered it freedom, a saner person's definition may have been "chaos."

After Daddy picked us up, our first stop was always Payless Drug Store, where he allowed us to pick out any toy our hearts desired. Then we'd head to his place, but not before making his usual pit stop to the liquor store. Daddy's drink of choice was Mr. Boston

Gin, straight out of the bottle. It went from his back pocket to his lips, and back again, throughout the day.

Whenever we asked him what he was drinking, although we had an idea, he'd always reply, "milk." As if we didn't know milk was not clear. One clue, in addition to the whispers we heard from Momma, was that whenever we got in the car with Daddy after he'd been drinking, he always took the back roads and instructed us to watch out for the police. This was before seat belt laws were enforced, and drunk driving laws were not nearly as strict. It's one of the many circumstances I have survived that I thank God for today. I count it a blessing that I am alive and healthy, while the horrific injuries and casualties of others who weren't quite so lucky under the same circumstances, led to the DUI laws that are enforced today.

Over the course of the weekend, we sometimes rode bikes or skated up and down the street with the neighborhood kids. Daddy bought my first two-wheeler from a garage sale when I was five. He taught me how to ride. Sometimes when he backed his car out the driveway, he would let me sit in his lap and steer the car with his oversized grip guiding my tiny little fingers. I can even remember a time or two going fishing with him in the wee hours of the morning. One of my favorite past-times with Daddy was when he would let me walk on his feet. He'd hold my hands while I faced him and hopped on his gigantic shoes. In Berkeley, at Aquatic Park, he taught my brother and me how to put together and fly our kites.

We also played tag, and hide and seek. Sometimes we invited friends over to Daddy's apartment and set up makeshift indoor tents using sheets, chairs, pillow cases, pillows, tables and chairs. Whatever worked, went into our tents. James was especially creative and talented in tent making. He would always create the biggest best tent, with separate rooms and entryways. His creativity is no wonder, as he is also a very gifted artist.

Once my father's two sisters, Aunt Pauline and Aunt Dorothy, who were much more astute, logical, and sober, came in town;

and when they saw the mess, they told him to have us clean up. He politely responded, "Leave those children alone, they're not bothering anyone." If at all possible, that just made me love him more. His two loving sisters would help him clean up the mess once we were gone. Later in his life, they would also take care of him when he was no longer able to care for himself.

On Saturday afternoons Daddy typically prepared a home cooked meal. I don't believe it was so much because we were there, but rather because he loved his own cooking. Nevertheless, he was a soul food connoisseur, and I also loved his cooking. He fixed everything from neck bones, ox tails, and pig feet, to grits, rice and gravy, cabbage, and corn.

When dinnertime rolled around at Mommas house, we knew it was going to be one of two things—Hamburger Helper or frozen TV dinners. Every now and then Momma would order a bucket of fried chicken, dinner rolls, and fries to be delivered to our door-step from a nearby restaurant, Chicken Delight. Their slogan was, "Don't cook tonight, call Chicken Delight."

As a child, I thought Momma couldn't cook. As an adult, I learned Momma was a culinary artist. When we were growing up, she was just too tired to cook. When I went to visit Momma as an adult, sometimes she'd be in the kitchen whipping up all kinds of dishes—from collard greens, black-eyed peas, fried corn, and pot roast, to smothered chicken, rice, and tossed salads. Her food melted in my mouth. There was also something about the way Momma arranged the food on her plate. She made everything look so delicious. We'd have the same thing on our plates, and somehow I always wanted hers.

In the evenings while at Daddy's we'd often go to the Coliseum Drive-in to catch a movie. When "Gone with the Wind" first came out, we saw it there. Daddy loved Westerns, Science Fiction, and James Bond movies. James loved Superhero movies. Usually, I was never interested in the movie, but just happy to be in Daddy's company for the weekend. Sometimes our friends got to come along with us. They called Daddy, "Uncle Jim." He'd give us all money, and send us to the snack bar to buy hot dogs, popcorn, pizza, and soda. Right outside the snack bar was a play area, equipped with swings, a slide, a spinner, and a teeter totter. We generally played there during intermissions, but sometimes, much to my delight, we'd play there for the entire movie.

Sometimes in the summer, Daddy, James and I would drive from Oakland to Los Angeles, where he was from, and where he had a lot of family. He told us that, in order for him to stay awake, we had to take turns rubbing his bald head…so we did. When I look back now, I think he just wanted his head massaged. From what I can remember, he never drank on the long trips, and we didn't have to watch out for the police. Although he wasn't as gregarious on these trips because he wasn't drinking, there was still no one else I'd rather be with.

On many occasions when we were in my father's care, after he was sure we were occupied, he would entertain scantily-clothed women in his bedroom. Some were no doubt prostitutes, and others were stray Caucasian hitchhikers. He'd pick these hitchhikers up on the side of the road whenever the opportunity availed, even while we were in the car. He entertained these women while we were outside playing with our friends. I remember, skating around the house once, playfully knocking on his bedroom window and running. Sometimes there were two men and one woman. The women often stole his money. On Fridays, prior to Daddy picking us up, Momma would debrief us to get his money before the women took it all.

None of this resonated with me as wrong. All I knew was that I loved my daddy, and I couldn't wait until Friday when he picked us up. Unbeknownst to me, his behavior with women would later inappropriately shape my attitude about sex, love, and intimacy in the future.

By the time we left on Sundays, his place was in total disarray. I'm sure it took at least a few days to get it all straightened back up—just in time for us to return the next Friday. When Daddy dropped us off on Sunday, as his soberness was kicking in, he and my mother would routinely argue. Most often, it was about child support; but sometimes it was about us coming home with missing pajamas, one shoe, mismatched socks, and other items we'd left behind.

At the time, I didn't realize that the reason Daddy was so much fun to be around on the weekend was because he was always drinking, and he was a "happy drunk." This took place from Friday evening to Saturday evening. We didn't understand that as children, we needed to have discipline, structure, and consistency. We lacked most of that at Daddy's. But there was consistency; that is, Daddy was consistently intoxicated on the weekends. By the time Sunday rolled around he was sobering up for the upcoming work week. When he was sober, he had a totally different personality. He was serious, easily agitated, and surly, especially toward my mother. Today I understand that the alcohol was his medicine, but I never completely understood the origin or the extent of his pain.

The first weekend that Daddy didn't pick us up is completely blocked from my memory. All I know is that I was 11-years-old, and we were still living on 61st Street in North Oakland. I don't even remember how I found out that Daddy had moved away. It's amazing how the brain works to protect us when things are too painful for us to handle. Unbeknownst to me, this was just the beginning of a long trail of people who would abandon me, before I was ready to let them go.

As innocent children, we didn't know that the fun we were having was a byproduct of highly dysfunctional parenting. Nor did we realize that the repercussions would follow us well into our adult lives, as we repeated the cycle and carried the dysfunction down to the next generation.

After Daddy left, during the most important developmental stages of my life, not only did I rarely see or hear from him anymore—but I never heard any more about my relationship to Booker T.

Washington. When I needed them the most, two very important men, connected to me by blood, went missing from the foundation of my life. Many years would go by before I saw Daddy again…and even more years would pass before I learned how my great-grandfather's work impacted history after the end of chattel slavery in America.

Success Principle Four—Interrupting Generational Cycles of Behavior

Children who are not properly parented, frequently grow up and repeat the same learned behaviors in their own households.

If they experienced their parents inflicting physical harm on one another, they are likely to grow up with violence in their home; if they experienced disrespect from their parents, they are likely to grow up disrespecting their children; if they experienced a lack of structure or stability, their children are likely to experience lack in those areas as well.

On the other hand, children thrive from respect, compliments, and trust. Show a child respect, and he or she will grow up to respect themselves and others. Compliment a child often, and he or she will grow up with confidence. Demonstrate to a child that you trust him or her, and they will grow up to be responsible.

Success Tips

❖ Intentionally seek out the good in children, and point it out to them often.

❖ Meet children where they are, and not where you want them to be, while magnifying their strengths and minimizing their weaknesses.

❖ Don't push children in directions that are clearly not a good fit for them, and instead encourage them in their positive interests.

"It often requires more courage to suffer in silence than to rebel, more courage not to strike back than to retaliate, more courage to be silent than to speak."
–Booker T. Washington

What I've Learned from my Great-Grandfather's life

I cannot learn as much by talking, as I can learn by listening—listening to others, listening internally, and listening in the stillness of meditation. I don't always have to speak to prove my point. If I have done something notable, the evidence will speak for itself.

Five
Pretty Is As Pretty Does

For as long as I can remember, I have frequently received compliments on my eyes and my smile. Some of the adjectives used to describe them include, captivating, pretty, beautiful, alluring, and even sexy. I couldn't have asked for two better ways to express my heart…through my smile and my eyes. No one could take that away from me. I have also been described as smart, more often than I can count.

I now realize that God blessed me with these qualities—a genuine smile, attractive eyes, and some level of intelligence. But I never fully, or partly for that matter, appreciated or recognized these qualities in myself while I was growing up. As an adult I took for granted that these attributes can be calming, inspiring, and uplifting for others because each attribute is naturally capable of imparting love, compassion, and wisdom—all factors that could change someone's life. Unfortunately, for many years of my young life, I was uncomfortable and insecure in my own skin, and I was intimidated by anyone who appeared to have the slightest bit of self-assurance.

As a little girl, Momma often said to me, "From the time you were born, I couldn't get through a store without someone stopping me to tell me just how pretty you were." She always said this in her usual facetious tone, as if she wanted to make sure I didn't become too vain. Later, when I was old enough to appreciate these compliments, Momma would humbly remark to me and to the person complimenting me, "Pretty is as pretty does."

I'm not sure why Momma thought this was a good child-rearing tactic, but I believe this was her humble attempt to keep me from becoming arrogant. From my childhood, and well beyond, no compliment ever went to my head. It took a lot for me to even believe a compliment. I thought at best, there was an ulterior motive behind every one given to me. Yet ironically, I thirsted for compliments in order to feel validated. When it came to what I thought of myself, my well was dry…and my self-esteem was low.

As one might imagine, while growing up I wasn't very outgoing or popular by any stretch of the imagination. I was a prime target for elementary school kids, who are honest at best and cruel at worst. The cruel ones enjoy nothing more than focusing on the flaws of the kids with poor self-esteem. This is what makes them feel good about who they are. In my case, they teased me about how my hand-me-down clothes were too small and/or didn't match, and how I spoke. Although I had never been to the South, I had a deep southern drawl, and I would drag my words. I inherited this from my mother who was born and raised in Tuskegee, Alabama. But in California, my dialect was foreign. I was often teased about this, and not only by kids, but by adults as well—adults who never learned as children, healthier ways to feel good about themselves.

Momma was not much for confronting issues like these head on. That is a trait I didn't inherit from her. Whenever I found out that someone said or did anything mean to my children, I gave them a tongue lashing that made that person wish they hadn't. I think Momma mostly just tried to wish problems away, hoping for a blissful life, free of any difficulties. Whenever I complained to her about the way the kids teased me, she pulled something out of her arsenal of clichés. Her response for this was, "Sticks and stones will break my bones, but words will never hurt me." She said that so often that I started reciting it to myself when the kids would attack me with their words. It didn't help much. Words did hurt me…and they left internal scars. The sadness I felt because of them would endure for a long time.

I couldn't do anything about the clothes I wore because I was too young to buy my own, and I couldn't do much about my accent. However, I could stop talking so they couldn't tease me. So, for a good part of my life, that's just what I did. Unless I was around someone who I believed loved me unconditionally—like a family member or a very close friend—I only opened my mouth to speak when it was absolutely necessary. I became quiet, shy, and reserved for many years.

In about the second grade, one of my classmates, Wanda, who was very confident and comfortable in her own skin, enjoyed bossing me around. Wanda's mother, who was our yard teacher during recess, was very nurturing and supportive of her daughter. Wanda was careful not to let her mother catch her doing anything mischievous. Hence, she thought of her daughter as an angel. However, feeding off of my low self-esteem, Wanda convinced me to do certain things for her; and I allowed her to boss me around.

Every time I did a task for Wanda, whether it was picking up something off the ground, or holding her sweater, I was humiliated at myself for the way I allowed her to treat me. I never realized that maybe I had the power to stop her. It wasn't that I was afraid of Wanda; I wasn't afraid of anybody. In fact, before I was old enough to know better, I used to think that if I was just given the chance, I could beat up Cassius Clay, aka Muhammad Ali. So, the fear wasn't that I couldn't hurt anyone physically. The fear was that I might hurt their feelings. When I was a child, no one ever bothered to tell me that what I felt mattered too. Instead, I was told, "Sticks and stones will break your bones, but words will never hurt you," and "Children are to be seen and not heard," and "Pretty is as pretty does." Thus, I thought I didn't deserve anything better, and I believed that this was just a part of normal life…at least for me.

The humiliation of sitting back quietly and allowing others to mistreat me became a theme in my life that I would carry well into my adult years. What started out with mean kids, advanced to others, including emotionally unavailable boyfriends, pretentious girlfriends, and backstabbing co-workers. I nursed their feelings at the expense of starving my own.

Be that as it may, there was one difference as I got older: I would take the mistreatment, but only for so long. Eventually when I could take no more, the "Pretty is as pretty does" drill went out the window, as I would suddenly blow up, making the person at hand pay for every last person who had ever had the audacity to mistake my kindness for weakness…or, who *I allowed* to mistake my kindness for weakness.

While I may have had the right to be angry, the way it came out was wrong, inappropriate, and oftentimes emotionally lethal. That surprised a lot of people, because on the outside, I appeared prim and proper with a quiet and reserved demeanor, soft eyes, and a pretty smile. Little did they know, on the inside, I was like a ticking time bomb waiting to blow. I verbally hit below the belt, looking for mean ways to psychologically hurt the person who hurt me first. If they were large in size, I talked about their weight. If their boyfriend cheated on them, I rubbed that in their face. If they were intellectually challenged, I let them know just how stupid I thought they were…*and don't let me put it in writing.* I was even more dangerous once I put pen to paper.

Unfortunately, I used the gift I had for writing to articulately tear a person down to a million little pieces. After all, I had years of training from watching and listening to my parents assassinate each other's character while I was growing up. Nevertheless, when all was said and done…and/or written, I felt twice as bad as I did when I was taking their mistreatment. My heart bled for the person. In addition to my initial humiliation from their mistreatment, now there were added feelings of guilt and shame. I also wrote my share of apology letters.

Though my childhood wasn't the one I would have chosen, there were some nice moments. My fondest memories with Momma mostly involved surprises that she, the tooth fairy, the Easter bunny, and Santa Claus gave to me. Once when I lost my tooth, the next morning, in addition to the small change under my pillow, there were three different color balloons held together with matching ribbon sticking to the wall like magic. I was beside myself with happiness. I later learned that was static electricity, but back then it was beyond explanation in my little mind.

While some believe making a cake from scratch shows more love than buying an already made cake, my mother was just the opposite. Though she never gave me a birthday party, she always made sure to pick up a birthday cake from Neldam's Danish Bakery on Telegraph Avenue in Oakland. My brother's birthday is March 26. I remember when I was around 8-years-old, and he was around 10-years-old, his birthday fell on Easter. My mother ordered a beautiful birthday cake for him, adorned with Easter decorations. Momma saw the disappointment and/or jealousy on my face. When she went to pick up his cake she bought me a small purple cake in the shape of an Easter egg. It was just for me, and I was in seventh heaven.

At Christmas time Momma would put our presents in the attic. When we finally fell asleep on Christmas Eve, she would place them carefully under our silver aluminum tree, in front of the spinning color wheel, which changed the tree from blue to red to green to orange, over and over again. One evening when Momma was asleep, James snuck in the attic to prove that she was the one supplying our gifts, and that no one would be coming on a sled with reindeers in the middle of the night. When he brought them out, I was devastated that Santa was not real.

The next day James said to Momma, using a smartass tone, "I know there's no such thing as Santa Clause." After it left his mouth, Momma's reply was unexpected. Calm and collected she replied, "Good, now I don't have to spend money on presents anymore." That was even more devastating than Santa not being real. Her words hit us both like a ton of bricks. Distraught, but thinking on my feet, I quickly went to her and said, with all the innocence I could muster up, "Momma, I still believe." That extended Santa Clause's life for me for about three more years.

Something else that I will always remember was the soap Momma brought home for us to use when we took our baths. It contained a surprise toy in the middle, and as the soap dissolved with each bath I could see the toy more and more clearly. After we got out of the bathtub, Momma would dry us off and lotion us down. Before we got in the bed she would kneel down with us and we'd say our prayers, "Now I lay me down to sleep, I pray the Lord my soul to keep. If I shall die before I wake, I pray the Lord my soul to take." Then we would bless as many people as we could possibly think of so that we could prolong our awake time before closing with, "Amen." And if I would try to fight my sleep, some-times she would brush my hair. That for me was like taking a tranquilizer. I loved when someone brushed, or played softly in my hair. My mom always reminded one of my baby sitters, Mrs. Doyle, that if she wanted me to go to sleep, all she had to do was brush my hair. That's just what Mrs. Doyle always did, and it worked every time.

Considering Momma always ingrained in me that "Pretty is as pretty does," and her mastery of the social graces was quite obvious, it's surprising that she smoked cigarettes. She also loved a good dirty Martini, and she knew everything about most sports, and was a diehard Oakland Raiders' fan…so diehard that when I was old enough to drive, Momma and I would go to the airport to welcome the team home after some of their playoff games. Then we'd drive away in a caravan with all of the other impassioned fans, all of us blowing our horns repeatedly. When the Raiders moved to Los Angeles in 1982, Momma was so heartbroken, that she disowned them for good.

For fun on the weekends, Momma would board a bus all by herself, and take a turn-a-round trip to Reno or Tahoe. Momma didn't drive so she would take a taxi cab to the Greyhound bus station. She'd leave early in the morning and return late the same night. It was only about a four hour drive one way. She wasn't a big gambler. This was just a source of pleasure for her. After she fed the quarters to the machine, she pulled the lever, and sat back with a cocktail in one hand and a cigarette in the other, hoping the cherries would all line up, and praying to hit a large jackpot. Often she would hit a small jackpot of a few hundred dollars. But, by the design of every casinos' execution plan, when she boarded the bus to return home, she had put all her winnings back in the slot machine.

Once when my father had a business trip scheduled, Momma decided that she was going to take James and me with her to the casino. We were going to be leaving early Saturday morning. We were excited. However, James did not follow her instructions to go to the barber shop after school that Friday. He had a huge afro, and he refused to get it cut. So Momma left him behind. He was about 14, and I remember feeling sorry for him because he didn't think she would really leave him, but she did. I can't remember who James stayed with; but I am pretty sure Momma didn't leave him home alone.

I was nowhere near old enough to be in a casino, but Momma didn't let that stop us. I would just stand around her at the slots until security kicked us out, and then we went to the next casino. There were more than enough to choose from. Somehow Momma discovered a kids' club at Harrah's casino in Tahoe where adults were not allowed. They could only come as far as the counter to sign their child in and out. That alone, was a thrill to me. The one time I went, I remember there were arcade games, board games, and lots of other activities to keep the children distracted while their caretakers were on the casino floor hoping to hit it big.

James and I were just two years apart, yet we were so completely different. Because he was a boy, the "Pretty is as pretty does" rule didn't apply to him. He was rebellious and I was cooperative. He would antagonize Momma, and I would adhere to whatever she wanted me to do. Our differences made me realize that two people, from the same parents, growing up together, in the same environment, can have two totally different attitudes about life. Just as no two people have the same thumbprint, we each develop a unique lens from which we see the world. As I grew older, understanding diverse characteristics would go a long way in my developing empathy, acceptance, and respect for the differences in all human beings.

My mother and her friends often doted over me—complimenting me about how smart I was; the creativity I expressed in the poems that I wrote; and how wisely I spent any money that was given to me. When I was 7-years-old, standing at the sink on a footstool in the kitchen, I can recall my mother talking to her girlfriend on the telephone, boasting about how thoroughly I washed the dishes, and how I properly faced the knives in a downward position in the dish drain. Though these moments are important in building a child's confidence, sadly, I don't remember my brother receiving any accolades from anybody for anything. Momma was often critical of James.

Momma repeatedly referred to James as incorrigible, exclaiming, "You're just like your father!" James was my father's namesake, which should be an honor bestowed on a child. Unfortunately for my brother, it seemed to have unavoidably placed him in dishonor with Momma. I think unconsciously for my mother, he was just a constant reminder of my father. My brother grew increasingly angry, which was understandable, but the way he channeled it was often inappropriate and unacceptable. When I think about it, I guess it was not too far removed from how I exhibited my anger as a young adult.

My estranged brother, Johnny, may have suffered the same fate because he was also a Jr. When I last saw him I was a little girl. I remember that at one time, he and two of our cousins, were adherent to the Islamic faith. They often wore suits and bow ties. Once they were in the kitchen attempting to make bean pies. It was obvious that they didn't know what they were doing when the bean pies, which were supposed to taste like sweet potato pies, tasted like beans. Johnny would pray five times a day. Once I knocked on the door while he was praying, and he screamed at me from the top of his lungs. Decades later, I now realize he had emotional issues at the very least; but when it happened, as a child I was afraid and ashamed at what I had done. It was just something else to add to the baggage I would carry through life.

Johnny later turned to drugs. He was always asking Momma for money. I recall him cursing at her and arguing with her often. The last I heard, Johnny was in Galveston, Texas. When Momma passed away in 1999 he called me once to find out about his share of the insurance money. When I said it was nice to hear from him after so many years, he replied coldly, "I am at the same number I've been at for the last 20 years." I sent his share of the money, and never heard from him again.

I wasn't close to any of my siblings except my brother James; and that was only because we were just two years apart, and we were raised together. He often teasingly referred to me as "Dee," Raj's pain-in-the-neck little sister from the 70's sitcom, "What's Happening." When we got along, we were good together. Unfortunately those times were too few and far between.

James and I would argue often. It makes sense, considering that is how our two closest adult role models commonly interacted with one another. The only difference with us is that, from as early as elementary school, our verbal fights frequently turned into physical bouts. To get us to stop Momma would come after us with the broom. We would routinely run from her and hide under the bed so she couldn't get to us. I didn't realize it then, but I know now that if Momma really wanted to hit us, she could have. Her idle threats seemed real at the time, and they were enough to get the two of us focused on something other than fighting. Neither of my parents ever actually spanked or hit me; so I can honestly say that amidst all of the other dysfunction I experienced as a child, I fortunately never saw or experienced physical abuse—at least not from either of my parents. Still, as James and I grew older our fights got worse.

When James was 14-years-old he began studying Islam. During this time, it was as if overnight he became more disciplined and very well-groomed. At that time he began referring to our White next-door neighbors as "the devil." They were a retired older couple who would always speak to us, and ask about school, or how our day was going. From my vantage point, their interest in our day, and the kindness they showed toward us appeared genuine. They often gave me and James small spending change when they saw us. One time, when I disagreed with him about them being devils, he abruptly threw a textbook and shattered a closed window in our home. I was completely stunned at not just his reaction, but also how his new found religion, though he appeared more disciplined, seemed to have created even more anger in him. Or perhaps his anger was just too deep to disappear overnight.

At the time, I had no idea what discernment was. But discernment told me then, and tells me now, that that couple was good. They helped shape my attitude in the future about people in general. Some were good, some were bad, and only time, and more importantly—their heart, would determine which they were—not the color of their skin. In order to promote how God intends for us to live, Martin Luther King, Jr.'s words, "I have a dream that my four little children will one day live in a nation where they will not be judged by the color of their skin, but by the content of their character," must apply in all ethnic directions.

Contrary to my brother's behavior, he planted a powerful seed in my Christian life long before I believed in Christ. Ironically, it happened around the same time that he began studying Islam. He has always been well-read, and very smart about many different issues, such as politics, history, and religion. One day I asked him, "Why do people believe in the Bible?" He answered, "Because things in the Bible that were prophesized have actually come true, and they continue to come to pass." It would be many years before I began practicing Christianity, but my brother's words definitely stayed with me. I now attempt to plant seeds back into his life.

As adults, my brother and I have had to intentionally undo a lot of the damage that was unintentionally done to us. For me, a huge part of that work has been learning to parent my own inner child. I have also come to believe that in her own way, Momma wanted me to know that I was pretty…but she was afraid of what might happen if it were to go to my head…if I were to take it in too deeply…or if I became too full of myself. She succeeded at making sure none of that happened. I was never anywhere near full of myself. In fact, I was mostly empty. She carried around her own self-doubt, and as she was my model, undoubtedly some form of this would trickle down to me and my own child-rearing practices.

Success Principle Five—Inner Beauty Spills over to the Outside

Before we can experience true outer beauty, our inner beauty must be intact. Our inner beauty can be seen on the outside through our attitude. Our attitude reflects how healthy our self-love is. Simply put, a bad attitude reflects poor self-love, and a good attitude reflects high self-love. Self-confidence is the end product of self-love. When we come to possess self-love we experience the true meaning of freedom.

When we do not carefully tend to self-love—daily, our self-esteem becomes damaged, especially when others tamper with it. But the good news is that the damage is never irreversible. The prerequisite for self-love is self-awareness, and learning to embrace our authentic self. In other words, it is being okay with who we are, despite what anyone else has said or done to us.

There will be times when we have to eliminate certain relationships in order to thrive in our self-love. Don't hold on to what's holding you back. Don't get caught up in feelings of hatred, anger or bitterness. Just let it go. As the saying goes, holding on to any one of these feelings is like taking poison and hoping your enemy will die.

Success Tips

- ❖ Don't be hard on yourself because you are not perfect—nobody is, but choose daily to be the best you, that you can be.

- ❖ Nurture your inner being consistently with meditation, relaxation, exercise, and good nutrition.

- ❖ Never compare yourself negatively against other people, because they also have flaws that are just different flaws from yours.

"I have learned that success is to be measured not so much by the position that one has reached in life, as by the obstacles which he has overcome while trying to succeed."
                                    –Booker T. Washington

What I've Learned from my Great-Grandfather's life

I cannot worry over everything that does not go as planned. I must trust the process as it unfolds, believing all things work out in the end. If I want others to recognize my external peace of mind, I have to first cultivate peace internally…and this is a daily practice.

Six

Invisible

We never had much in terms of clothes, housing, and food; and I can't say that these things were replaced by a consistent loving, nurturing home environment. When life is rich in those areas you won't notice what you lack. Because of the deprivation I experienced in all of these needs, growing up I often felt invisible to myself and to the outer world.

From the time I began elementary school, until my young adult years, I would look in the mirror and see a vision that disappointed me. To many of my classmates, I was not an authentic African-American. My skin was fair, my hair was fine and wavy, and my eyes were light brown, bordering on hazel, like my father's. Because of Daddy's brown skin tone he was unmistakably African-American. Because of my light skin, I often felt like an outcast.

As mentioned, my great-great-grandmother, Jane, was a victim of rape by a White man on a nearby plantation, who was suspected to be Booker T. Washington's father. Back then, babies born with any ounce of Black blood in them were considered Black, and thereby worthless. My great-grandmother, Olivia Davidson Washington, was also quite fair-skinned, and undoubtedly also a child of a slave woman who was raped. Both of my great-grandparents had strong European genes that were passed down through three generations; and as I would later learn, I was on the receiving end.

Skin color issues have always disappointed me. These issues don't only occur when it comes to other ethnic groups discriminating against Blacks, but I have learned that issues also arise within my own African-American race. For many years, this race question has haunted me. It started on my first day of school at Washington Elementary in North Oakland, a predominantly African-American public school. A day hardly went by that someone wasn't asking me, "What are you mixed with?" They would never accept that I was not mixed with anything.

We often miss the silver lining of having so many beautiful hues within our ethnicity. Instead, we are distracted and divided as we concentrate on light skin versus dark skin, not to mention the differences between our straight hair, wavy hair, and coarse hair. This has played out for me personally throughout my life, and I was tired of having to defend myself and explain to my own people that I was Black. It was just another blow to my already low self-esteem. Even as an adult, I continue to get asked the question, "What are you mixed with?" After so many times of responding, "Black," and getting comments and looks of unbelief, it has become frustrating and very uncomfortable for me. Yet, I wasn't about to lie to satisfy their unbelief. To disown my race would be to disown the privilege of the remarkable inner-strength and the soulful essence intrinsic in Black people. This wasn't something I was taught. It was a deep inherent feeling, permanent and inseparable from who I was, and who I am.

Like Momma, who was at least a shade or two lighter than me, I was too proud to deny being Black. In fact, it was somewhat comical whenever we were treated rudely in a public setting, Momma would always say, "They are only treating us like this because we're Black." And I would always respond, "Momma they don't even know you're Black," to which she would politely ignore. All I know, and am proud to state, is that on my birth certificate, in the ethnicity column it reads: Mother: Negro and Father: Negro.

It disappoints me that some African-Americans feel that light-skinned African-Americans should sometimes take a back seat. I would have welcomed being dark-skinned, and having an afro like my brother and most of my friends. Unfortunately, that's not what God had in mind when He created me, and there's nothing I can do about that. I dare say it's just as frustrating being a light-skinned African-American as it is being a dark-skinned African-American—both experience unacceptance at some level. Though there are many stories about dark-skinned Blacks with coarse hair, desiring to be lighter with straighter hair; but it was just the opposite for me. I desired so much to have dark skin. Or, at least to have an offspring with beautiful brown skin.

Langston Hughes, beautifully depicts in his poem, "Harlem Sweeties" an exquisite array of the different skin colors of African-American women. His description of the different skin tones, include, sepia, cream, chocolate, cinnamon, caramel, brown sugar, honey gold, peach, coffee, walnut, cocoa, bronze, and blackberry. It brings to my mind a majestic and rare quilt; something to be amazed with, instead of something that creates conflict and division.

After the curiosity about my skin tone, came the fascination with my hair. Some defined it as, "fine, delicate and soft, like angel hair." They could not resist touching it. Some wanted to brush it. They referred to it as "good hair," as if all that was left for them was "bad hair."

To make matters worse, though Momma's hair was a bit coarse, she was even lighter than me. I was embarrassed when she would walk me to school because the kids would tease me, calling my mother "that White lady." Or referring to me as "half and half," and "Oreo cookie." It was only when my mother would open her mouth to speak that her blackness came through. She was well-spoken, with a posh southern drawl, and a soulful inflection full of the type of substance that is not easily explained, and uniquely identified with Black people.

When I was 9-years-old James Brown came out with, "Say it Loud, I'm Black and I'm Proud." The lyrics, the feeling he added to the words, and the beat, rang through to the deepest parts of my soul. I was so proud to be Black. But the song only reinforced the negative feeling I had about the way I looked. I was disappointed that people always questioned my ethnicity. Most believed I was Black, but not one hundred percent Black.

There was nothing I desired more than to have a dark complexion with coarse hair, and a brown skinned mother; but, these were things I could do nothing about. I wanted a huge afro like my brother James—so desperately in fact, that I allowed my friend who had a beautiful afro, to put vinegar, beer, mayonnaise, and other ingredients in my hair and roll it up overnight with pink sponge curlers. When that didn't work we tried a new concoction, always to no avail. It came close a few times…but the end results were always the same. It just wouldn't stand up in the middle. My 'fro would flop and lay down on the sides, with frizzy ends.

Even though I was teased about everything from my mother's skin color, to my clothes, which more often than not, didn't match or fit properly, to the way that I talked, school still provided a positive outlet for me because my teachers always liked me. And I liked my teachers. Somehow I was always able to gain their favor. "Teacher's Pet" was an ongoing reality for me. Perhaps it was my natural inclination to respect them. Or maybe it was because the importance of getting an education was drilled in me from a very early age.

I'll never forget practicing for a dance routine with about sixty other students at Washington Elementary in the school cafeteria, which doubled as an auditorium. We were in four single file rows, each row made up of around fifteen students. The teacher pulled me out of the back of the row, and moved me to the front of one of the rows because I was doing so well. I felt so special. But I was careful that no one knew how special I felt because my mother's words, "Pretty is as pretty does," rang loud and clear in my head. That sound overpowered my feelings.

In elementary school I also tried playing the flute and the violin. Nothing came of it. No one pushed me or urged me on. I really liked to write poems too. Momma would brag about them. Somehow that flame also flickered out. Perhaps if I had known about my great-grandfather's rise above slavery, that alone would have been enough to encourage me to excel in any one of those artistries.

Booker T. Washington's only daughter, Portia, was still alive when I was in elementary school. Although my mother was very close to her Aunt Portia, I never met my great aunt. She was an accomplished pianist. Booker T. Washington arranged for her to attend New England's finest boarding schools, including Framingham State Normal School in Massachusetts. After grammar school she returned home to take classes at Tuskegee Institute, and in 1901 she attended Wellesley College in Massachusetts. In New England Portia continued her piano studies and she was the first African-American to receive a degree from the Bradford Academy, today known as Bradford College. Upon graduation Portia traveled to Berlin to study under Martin Krause, master pianist and former student of Franz Liszt.

From as early as I can remember, until the age of 12, my mother was granted a two-week respite from her single parenting duties, and James and I experienced a better lifestyle. It happened each summer when we went to Los Angeles to visit Momma's youngest sister, Gloria Washington Jackson and her husband, Dr. Theodore Jackson, who we referred to as Aunt Gloria and Uncle Pete. They had three daughters and two sons, who were my older cousins. Uncle Pete was a prominent surgeon, with a thriving private practice. During the summer, when their three daughters were in high school, they made extra money by working in his office. Once in a while they would give me chores to do around the office. I admired each of my girl cousins. Growing up, I wanted to be them.

When James and I arrived at their house, we likely had on our usual mismatched clothes, and appeared somewhat deprived. Without Daddy giving Momma child support, it was difficult at best to keep us in new clothes, especially while we were consistently growing out of them. It was hard to do "pretty" in my wardrobe...but despite my flaws, my cousins always managed to make me feel like a little sister.

Their lifestyle was pretty much the opposite from ours. Although Aunt Gloria was the youngest of my mother's younger three sisters, she always appeared to me to be the wisest and most sensible. Maybe it was because she was the only one of her sisters who was still married to her first husband, and they raised five children in an intact family. The Jacksons lived in a huge three-story home, with a swimming pool and fruit trees aligning the yard. Their home was located in Windsor Hills, a well-to-do African-American community. They had a huge Collie named Biff. Momma used to tell me that Biff would watch over me when I was a baby, but I don't know if that was quite true. They even had a housekeeper. I loved being at their home; compared to ours, it was a castle.

I'd heard that Uncle Pete purchased the house in the 1940s for a mere $40,000. When they first moved there, it was a predominately White community, and someone spray painted "NIGGER" on the garage door. It's amazing how things change with courage and time. Today that same neighborhood is bustling with thriving upper echelon African-American families, including physicians, judges, engineers, successful entrepreneurs, and celebrities.

Each summer while I was with them, I would go school shopping with the girls. We went to store, after store, after store, and all I can remember them looking at, and buying, were blue jeans. After what seemed like hours of driving and shopping, they would arrive back home with at least ten pair of jeans between them. I'm sure there was something different and stylish about each pair, but to my inexperienced eye, they all looked the same. After all, the only time I ever went school shopping was once with my Aunt Margaret.

The Jacksons always took vacations together during the summer. If we were lucky their vacation was scheduled during the two weeks James and I would be there. We often went with them on trips to lakes, resorts, and national parks. They had a motor boat, and each of my cousins would take turns water skiing on the back, while I rode on the inside, enjoying myself immensely, with the wind blowing through my hair and the water splashing on my face. On the trips when we didn't go out of town with them, we frequently went to Disneyland.

There were pool parties at their home. I remember one in particular. Stevie Wonder's, "I Was Made to Love Her," was playing full blast in the background, while my cousins and all of their friends were playing, singing, and dancing in the pool. I was the smallest one in the bunch, and the only one unable to swim. I was riding on a raft, and having a good time too. That is, until someone, who was unaware that I couldn't swim, pulled the raft from under me and I nearly drowned. Needless to say, I survived; but after that, I never wanted to learn to swim. *Today learning to swim is on my bucket list.*

Sometimes my oldest cousin, Bonnie, would take me with her to watch her boyfriend, Michael Beale, practice with a new band at one of the band member's parent's home. Although I didn't know it at the time, this turned out to be a highlight of the trip. I remember going to one of the band's first concerts where they were the opening act. We sat very close to the stage, probably VIP seats... but I don't remember. The music was loud and full of electrifying energy. The band members were all over the place, dancing, jumping, and even rolling on the stage floor as they played their instruments and harmonized vocally with precision and excellence. They were amazing. The audience was going crazy. Today that little known group, Earth Wind and Fire, is inducted in the Grammy Hall of Fame.

The youngest girl, Adrienne, was like a big sister who I had a love/hate relationship with. She would take me on all kinds of adventures in her sports car, from showing me Berry Gordy's and Ray Charles's homes in a nearby affluent community, to chasing her boyfriend as he fled away from her with someone else. She always had the most charming and attractive boyfriends, and she was charming and attractive too. Although I was three years her junior, I had a crush on whoever she was dating. Truth be told, out of the three sisters, I most wanted to be her. She was full of personality. Some of her friends wanted to be like her too. They emulated her clothes and hairstyles, and mimicked her lingo. She was a natural leader.

Sometimes while at the Jacksons' home, I just wanted to be by myself. They were all older, and although I loved and adored each of my cousins, some of the things that interested them, didn't interest me at all. One particular evening, I went in the living room to watch television on their large floor model console TV. As I relaxed comfortably, sitting Indian style on the floor in the living room, my Uncle Pete came into the room, and he asked me in a stern, yet curious tone, "What are you doing in here? Nobody else is down here. Why aren't you upstairs with everybody else?" Immediately I stood up and walked quickly upstairs with, what felt like "my tail between my legs."

I'm sure Uncle Pete did not realize how hard his words hit me. After all, without his buy-in it's doubtful that James and I would have been there two weeks each summer, not to mention accompany them on vacations. He was a responsible father and husband, and it wasn't his fault that my father was not. He had no idea how fragile I was, and how ashamed I felt. The words hit me like a ton of bricks. Although these weren't his words at all, what I heard in my delicate state was, "Who do you think you are?!" That was just one more experience I'd add to my baggage.

The next best thing to spending weekends with Daddy, or visiting my cousins in Los Angeles, was going to visit my friend, Teresa's house, at the opposite end of the block in North Oakland. She was about two years younger than me, which seemed like a decade, when I was 9-years-old. She was an only child, and lived with her mother and grandmother in a nice two-story home. Everything around her was neat and clean. Her mother and grandmother cherished her. I never knew what it was like to have real grandparents, and I thought about how lucky she was to live with one of hers. There was always the aroma of a home cooked meal being prepared in Teresa's kitchen. Once in a while I was allowed to stay and bake cookies with her and her mother. It was during this time in my life, when I first heard the term "Don't wear out your welcome." Momma would often yell it out when I was happily skipping on my way down to Teresa's house.

Teresa had every toy a girl could ever want, including many Barbie dolls and all of the Barbie accessories imaginable—the house, the car, tons of Barbie's shoes and clothes, and even a Ken. In her backyard, there was a swing and slide set, among the apricot and apple trees. To me, this was like the Garden of Eden and she lived in Heaven. At my suggestion, we would often play house in my friend's backyard. We always had husbands and children, and my friend would always play along with me; but I don't think that she really wanted to. I am not sure what my fascination was with it. Perhaps it helped me to imagine a better life.

Though she and her mother and grandmother welcomed me, I can't say that I ever remember them initiating the visits. Invited or not, it was a welcome change from my reality at the other end of the block, where life was completely different.

Success Principle Six—Don't allow others to define you

When we possess a healthy sense of confidence we can stand up for ourselves without violating others. In this sense, confidence is a requirement for maintaining healthy relationships. Often it is the insecurities within, which cause our relationships to break down. More importantly, our insecurities often lead to letting others define who we are.

Understanding who we are, who we truly are, helps our confidence fall into place. Once this occurs, we don't need to put others down, or see others suffer, in order to feel good about ourselves, or our circumstances. Nor do we need approval from others to feel good about who we are.

Gaining confidence is a matter of taking confidence back. We begin to develop confidence when we are very young. At the same time, confidence begins to get stripped, and our spirits become broken, when we are very young. As children we are not in a position to do much about it. But as we grow older, it is our responsibility to take control, and get our confidence back.

Success Tips

❖ Never dwell on someone else's negative opinion of who they think you are, because what you focus on, you feed, and what you feed…grows.

❖ Self-confidence is something you can breed with positive self-talk, being around people who have your best interest at heart, and by weeding out those who don't.

❖ Decide on how you want others to positively characterize you, and put together an action plan to maintain, and/or, cultivate those traits within yourself.

"There are two ways of exerting one's strength; one is pushing down, the other is pulling up."

—Booker T. Washington

What I've Learned from my Great-Grandfather's life

If I get down in the trenches with others and help to pull them out, I am much more effective than if I tell them how to get out. As one saying goes, "People don't care how much you know, until they know how much you care."

Seven
Shattered Villages

Although our North Oakland neighborhood was decent, our home was not. We lived in an unkempt four room flat on the top floor of a single family home that was turned into a duplex. Upon opening the front door to our unit, there were around 21 stairs leading up to the entry hallway. There was a living room, and kitchen for sure. The other two rooms seemed somewhat makeshift. James and I slept in twin beds in the front room, which Momma made into a bedroom, and she slept on the pullout couch in the living room. Our house was usually a mess.

There were a couple of unhappy memories, in particular, that occurred when we lived on 61st Street. These memories reinforced the unhealthy thinking about intimacy that my father's behavior with women had already planted in my head. The first occurred when I was around 9-years-old, and the paperboy, who was at least six years older than I was, invited me to ride on his handle bars on his route around the corner. When he came to a bluish grey stucco, four unit apartment building he beckoned for me to follow him inside to a stairwell. He sat on the steps and exposed himself, and then put my hand on his penis. On some level I knew there was something wrong with what happened, but I chalked it up to all else in my life that wasn't okay. Although it wasn't okay, it was normal for me. At that time, I hadn't a clue that I deserved a lot better. All I remember after touching him is that he swore me to secrecy, and I never said a word to anyone. The rest of that day is repressed. I don't even remember leaving the building or going home.

The next incident occurred after my father moved away, when I was 11-years-old. As I was walking home from my friend's house at the opposite end of our block, our landlord, who appeared old as dirt, offered me a ride home in his old dilapidated truck. I trusted him. He and his wife owned the property where we lived. His wife was a very kind and gentle woman who seemed too nice and polished for him. When we arrived in front of my house, he stopped the truck, leaned over close to my ear, and said in a low voice, "One day I am going to pick you up and take you somewhere and you can't tell anyone…you hear?" I nodded in agreement and hopped out of the truck. Again, I knew something wasn't right about what he said, but this time I decided to tell Momma…maybe because he was so old…maybe because he was married. I guess that was Momma's breaking point because I never in my life saw her get so mad. She turned red with anger. Though his act was terrible, her reaction validated her love for me. I asked her not to say anything, but to no avail. She told him off in no uncertain terms, and threatened to tell his wife. He never bothered me again. But, after that, I was very uncomfortable whenever I saw him. We would stay there for a while longer, probably because the neighborhood was decent, the rent was low; and it was near Momma's job, our baby sitter, and our school. I am almost certain, though, that this incident contributed to our eventual move.

In North Oakland, across the street from us in a modest upstairs apartment on the corner, lived Uncle Barney. He wasn't my real uncle, but he was like the brother Momma never had. Barney Hilburn was the first black man to hold elected office in Oakland. He was elected to the Board of Education from School District 3 on April 21st, 1959. At the time I was only 2-months-old. He was considered influential in the hiring of Marcus Foster, Oakland Unified School District's first Black superintendent. He was also a school board president at one time. Uncle Barney passed away in 1990.

Momma would always volunteer on his campaigns. James and I were involuntary workers as well. Momma also volunteered on political campaigns and other causes she believed in. She happily went about passing out literature, answering telephones, making calls, or doing anything else that was needed. I remember at least once or twice walking with Momma through our neighborhood, knocking on doors to raise money for the March of Dimes.

Uncle Barney was another one who would rave about how smart I was. Although my brother was the oldest, he'd always make me responsible for the pocket change he'd give to us. He said I would do the right thing with it, and suggested my brother would not. No doubt these words helped shape me into an independent thinker later in life; but if that's the case, how would it impact my brother's future? This is just one example of how the ball was unintentionally dropped by us, within our community, without our awareness. However, I believe the ball is still within reach for the countless children, teens, and adults, who have fallen prey to these unintended messages.

Uncle Barney and Momma had a friend in common. Her name was Effie. She was originally from Beaumont, Texas. Effie had a sister, Louise, who we all knew by her nickname, Tooten. Both sisters had deep dark chocolate skin, petite frames, high chiseled cheekbones, and short afros. They both had no-nonsense attitudes. Although they were small in stature, they didn't take any mess from anybody. The two sisters were very close, and they came as a package deal, but Momma was closest to Effie.

In common they were all from the south, and they all liked to drink and let go of their inhibitions. In every other way, it seemed that the two of them were in sharp contrast to Momma. My mother was college educated and a member of a sorority, they were not. They loved to cook and clean, Momma did not. They were feisty. Momma was polished and poised. They were a little rough around the edges. Momma was prim and proper. Momma loved to talk about politics and sports. They could care less about either. Momma was crazy about jazz. They'd rather listen to soul, R&B, and blues.

One of the biggest contrasts was that they each kept a loaded revolver in the nightstand by their bed. My mother would cringe at a picture of a gun, no less the thought of owning one. I'm not sure what went on in those days or with their environment in North Oakland that made them feel more secure with a loaded gun nearby. Perhaps it was an attitude they brought from Texas. Today, nearly 45 years later, it would seem to make a lot more sense to have a gun with all of the senseless crime, and the murder rate in Oakland.

Another sharp contrast was the language they used. Despite the fact that I credit both sisters with teaching me proper table etiquette, including how to properly hold my knife and fork, and how to cut meat with my knife; and good social manners, including responding with yes, please, thank you, and no thank you…they cursed like sailors. It took an extreme amount of frustration before Momma would utter the words, *damn* or *shit*. That was as far as I'd ever heard her go. She chalked cursing up to a limited vocabulary and bad grammar, and Momma never missed an opportunity to correct poor grammar. Nevertheless, for a time, Momma and Effie were inseparable.

One would think that it was my mother who would have taught me all of the manners and etiquette I needed to know. But she was even quiet in that area. Even so, I did learn much, just by watching her. She was a walking demonstration of the social graces…the way she held a glass…the way she sat…and the way she greeted others, just to name a few. But it was her two feisty friends from Texas, who insisted there were certain behaviors that James and I would display…and there were others that we would not display.

When I first met them I was 5-years-old. That's when I began calling them Aunt Tooten and Uncle Effie. Uncle Effie was not gay by any stretch of the imagination. I endearingly used the term "Uncle" because of an incident which occurred one day while she was driving and I was in the back seat of her car. I innocently called her by her first name because I wanted to find out where we were going; and in a strong disciplinary voice, she said, "In no uncertain terms will you ever call me Effie. You can call me Miss Effie, Mrs. Effie, Mr. Effie, Aunt Effie, or Uncle Effie, but you will not call me Effie!" Although I now believe she was being sarcastic with "Mr. Effie, and Uncle Effie," at 5-years-old I wanted to see what she would do if I said Uncle Effie. So, I said, "Okay, I'll call you Uncle Effie." And the rest is history. The name stuck and took on a life of its own. Not only did I call her Uncle Effie, but everyone else; children and adults alike, began to affectionately deem her, Uncle Effie. Although some may think that calling her "Uncle" is a sign of disrespect, but for me, that was the first of many lessons she and Aunt Tooten would teach me about respecting my elders.

Uncle Effie and Aunt Tooten kept their homes immaculate. Something that Aunt Tooten said that I have followed as an adult, was, "I can't stand to cook in a dirty kitchen." And they were both always grilling, baking, broiling, or frying something. From seafood gumbo, to links and ribs, to freshly caught fish, which the men caught and scaled, and they cleaned and cooked. They had never been or desired to go to a fast food restaurant. They even churned homemade ice cream. Their famous words at the table were, "If it's on your plate, you better eat it. If you don't want it, don't get it."

Aunt Tooten could make a delicacy out of anything. Her specialty was beef kidneys, smothered in gravy and onions. The first time I saw her make them, I was grossed out. After they were done she insisted that I at least taste them before determining that I didn't like them. She said, "I lived through the Great Depression, and this is how we got through it...you never know when something may happen and you have to resort to inexpensive meals." Reluctantly I put a small portion in my mouth, and they were irresistible. From then on, I would often ask her to make them. As we ate that day, she explained how living through the Great Depression forced them to make ends meet as best they could with very little money. *An explanation goes a long way with a child.*

Uncle Effie adored me from the day we first met; and I adored her because I could genuinely feel her love. She kissed and hugged me often. She affectionately gave me nicknames, like, Gravel Girtie and Sadie Lou. When I would playfully tease her about something she did, like dancing or singing, she'd sometimes call me a heifer, which is a slang term for a young cow. She actually pronounced it, "heffa." As strange as it may seem, even this seemed like an extension of her affection, first because of the playful way she said it, and second because of the amount of love she shared with me, and the attention she showered upon me.

Though Momma was a workaholic during the week, on the weekends she usually made time for fun with her girlfriends. If Daddy was on a business trip, we went along with Momma. Uncle Effie and Aunt Tooten were firm believers that when adults were entertaining company, children were to be "seen and not heard." I understand that more, now that I am an adult. At best, today we have to curve our conversation because we've dropped the ball on children being in the same room with adults who are letting their hair down. At worst, we don't even curve the conversation. But for my mother and her friends, the sky was the limit. Every once in a while they would come in the room they had set up for us to make sure we were okay. Sometimes if we were being too loud, or playing too rough for them, they would jokingly say to us, "Go play on the freeway." Or they might threaten us by saying they were going to get their pistols. Of course, they never would.

The only time we were allowed to come in the same room where the adults were, was if they called us. This was usually when they offered us a dollar to show them the latest dance moves. For some reason, although we were dying inside to show off what we could do, they usually had to beg us for a good ten minutes before we gave in. After about thirty seconds of dancing, we got our money and ran back to the room. They went back to talking, gossiping, laughing, and drinking cocktails…all while listening to their favorite tunes on the stereo until the wee hours of the night.

Momma was a serious jazz fan, but she would forego her jazz for her friends. They liked soul music, blues, and R&B from the likes of Bobbie Womack, Marvin Gaye, Diana Ross, B.B. King, Bobby Blue Bland, Bobbie Womack, and Aretha Franklin. Momma preferred Dizzie Gillespie, Miles Davis, Oscar Peterson, Ella Fitzgerald, and Sarah Vaughn, to name a few. She even liked a little Brazilian bossa nova, like "The Girl from Ipanema."

Their elderly father, Papa Daddy, lived with Aunt Tooten. Papa Daddy was a very frail man with only one arm. The other was missing at the elbow, leaving a stub. For that reason, I was never able to get too close to him. I was afraid. But Papa Daddy was very nice and quiet, unless he was explaining something, which always seemed to be something deep. He had no formal education, but Uncle Effie said that he taught himself how to read, and he read everything he could. Aunt Tooten and Uncle Effie adored their father, and they said he was the wisest man they'd ever met. There weren't many questions about history, geography, or astronomy that he didn't know the answer to.

In so many ways, Uncle Effie and Aunt Tooten positively shaped my life. Two older Black women who lived on limited incomes, and lacked higher education. They set examples by keeping well-maintained homes; preparing home cooked meals, three times a day, nearly every day of the week; disciplining us with love and care; teaching us table manners; and how to be polite and show respect for our elders.

Uncle Effie and Momma stopped speaking when I was still young. I am not sure why, but I think my mother had to try too hard around them to be someone she wasn't. Although it was easy to love Uncle Effie, I believe she and my mother were just too different. Uncle Effie lacked the prominent upbringing, educational background, and the social connections my mother had. She was not accepted in the same social circles as my mother.

Or it may have been because of Uncle Barney. Once I overheard my mother talking to someone on the phone about how Uncle Effie had eyes for him, and how she was using my mother to get close to him. Momma went on to say that she believed Uncle Barney was attracted to Uncle Effie, and liked her feistiness, but he ran in political circles with highly educated people, and she was not the type of woman he'd be comfortable with in those settings.

Eventually the alcohol and the camouflage from my mother's reality was not enough to hold Momma and Uncle Effie together. I missed Uncle Effie so much. Years later, when I was a teenager, Momma got a call from Aunt Tooten. Uncle Effie had terminal cancer. That's when I witnessed a very loving side of Momma as she often went to Uncle Effie's bedside to comfort her until she passed away. When Uncle Effie died I felt as if a part of me died with her. No other adult demonstrated love toward me quite the way that she did. It's over forty years ago, but every year since, on her birthday, February 4, I think about her.

Momma's younger sister, Margaret Washington Clifford, lived not too far from us in Oakland. We spent a lot of time visiting her.

Aunt Margaret was the most creative person I have ever met. My mother and my Aunt Gloria often raved about the clothes Aunt Margaret made for them, including prom and wedding dresses. My mother said some of the gowns she made were even reversible, formal and glamorous on both sides.

Momma, James, and I spent a lot of time with her. She always marveled at my progress in school. There is only one time in my life when I ever went school shopping, and that was with Aunt Margaret, when I was around 9-years-old. I can remember picking out my new clothes in the, long since demolished, MacArthur shopping center in North Oakland.

Christmas time was always special for us at Aunt Margaret's house. Taking off where her mother (my grandmother) Edith Meriwether Washington left off, she took over the Washington Candy Company, which my grandmother started in her home in Tuskegee. Around October, Aunt Margaret started making tons of candy and fruit cakes. By December, she shipped professionally wrapped boxes of candy, and round tin containers of fruit cakes all over the country, to people who ordered far in advance to give as gifts for their friends and family. When she wasn't looking, James and I couldn't resist the temptation to sneak the candy. The fruit cake was always safe because we hated it. But we loved the candy. We ate so much of it that our terrible stomach aches were always a dead giveaway.

Every year, from as early as I can remember, until I was around 12-years-old, we went with her to pick out the most beautiful white flock Christmas tree she could find. After she finished decorating the tree with different blue ornaments, she'd turn on the spinning color wheel, and the white tree would change colors. At dusk, James and I would pile into her seemingly gigantic 1960s station wagon with the brown wood side paneling. Aunt Margaret could parallel park that car like nobody's business. I'd watch in amazement as she wedged into the smallest parking spaces. We would drive all over Oakland, from the flat lands to affluent neighborhoods in the Oakland hills, to see the fabulous Christmas lights and the decorations.

There was no end to Aunt Margaret's brilliant creativity. Whether it was making candy or clothes, or decorating Christmas trees, she was a master. It seemed effortless for her to create anything. She learned to sew and cook when she lived in Tuskegee. Those were just a couple of vocations Booker T. Washington (her grandfather) advised his first students, who were former slaves, to take on in hopes that they would excel in the latest developments in the industry, and turn these skills into gainful businesses of their own. He once said, "The individual who can do something that the world wants done will, in the end, make his way regardless of his race."

My cousin Robin, Aunt Margaret's youngest of three children and only girl, was another perk of visiting Aunt Margaret. Robin is nine years older than me. She took me under her wing when I was a little girl. To my delight, when she lived in Oakland, Robin babysat me on occasion. I was Robin's little protégé. She always gave me sound practical advice. It was because of Robin that later in my life I would earn a bachelor's degree in business. She said this was a degree that would be very useful. It proved to be sound advice when I graduated, and it still holds true today.

From her, I also learned the importance of not going anywhere unkempt. You never know who you might run into. I missed the mark many times. I can't recall how many times her image has gone through my mind when I've run out of the house somewhat flawed, and bumped into someone who used to like me, or perhaps I used to have a crush on, or a rival female schoolmate, at the most inopportune moment. Robin never went anywhere without putting on makeup—even if it she was just going to make a quick run to the corner store and back home.

What I remember most about my younger years with Robin, is how much fun she was to be around. When we'd go anywhere in the car, at every stop light, she'd make the car dance to the beat of whatever music was playing on the radio. At 8-years-old, that was by far the coolest thing I'd ever witnessed. I was so in awe of my cousin. She was confident and beautiful, and she had the best personality of anyone I'd ever met. In my eyes, Robin appeared flawless.

Sometimes Aunt Margaret and Robin didn't see eye to eye. I was in elementary school when Robin left Oakland to go to Tuskegee to live with our grandmother. I was ecstatic whenever she came back to Oakland.

My mother worked a lot, so during the week we spent a great deal of time with our babysitter, Mrs. Henry, who we automatically came to refer to as, Grandma. Her home was one of the few places I would go as I was growing up, where there was a sense of normalcy, structure, and consistency. She lived with her husband, Mr. Henry, who we deemed Grandpa. The Henrys lived just a few doors down the street from us on 61st Street. They were the only grandparents I ever knew because with the exception of my maternal grandmother, they had all passed away before I was born. My maternal grandmother died when I was very young, and in elementary school; and because she lived in Tuskegee, I didn't remember her. My mother said when I was born she came to visit us in California and she would rock me to sleep every night while she was there. I never knew either of my father's parents, or heard much about them, other than occasional snide remarks my mother would make about my father's mother.

The arguing and unkind words that we were accustomed to from our parents did not occur at Grandma and Grandpa's house. There was also never a hint of any alcohol or cigarettes, which were commonplace in our house. Grandma always appeared well-put together. Her grey hair shined beautifully through her natural golden tint. She always kept her hair in a thick, neatly braided bun.

Grandpa was a quiet, respectful man. He was a Pullman Porter for Amtrak, so he was often away. Grandma was a deaconess and Grandpa was a deacon. When Grandpa was home, they spent a lot of time at their church. The only time James and I attended church as children was with them; and it was usually during the week because we spent most weekends with Daddy. Grandpa had a light green 1950s Chevrolet. In my little mind, it appeared gigantic. My brother and I would climb into the back, and sink into the seat. I'd look up, and the ceiling of the car seemed to be quite a distance from our little bodies.

When Grandpa was home, he and Grandma would sit across from each other in the living room, in vintage chairs by the window. They would quietly study their Bibles around the same time in the evening. Although it would take several more seeds, they dropped the very first one that would lead me to God much later in my life.

Like Uncle Effie and Aunt Tooten, their home was immaculate. The furniture was always polished with not a speck of dust anywhere. The house always smelled of lemon pledge, unless there was something in the kitchen cooking. Grandma and Grandpa had diabetes, so it was always a healthy meal. For some reason, the meatloaf with rice and gravy and salad sticks out in my mind. It was delicious. Grandma's home cooked meals were always a welcome change from the Hamburger Helper or T.V. Dinners James and I ate nearly every night during the week.

Grandma was very wise, sensible and practical. She didn't allow us to watch too much television. To this day, I don't care for shows such as Batman and Superman because she ingrained in me that it was plain foolishness. Somehow that same idea didn't sink in with my brother. He would pretend to be one of the superheroes at recess, along with his good friends, Curtis and Billy.

I often followed Grandma to tend to her garden in the backyard. It was very well-manicured, and it was the most colorful home garden I had ever seen. There were varietals of purple, pink, lavender, orange, red, yellow, and white flowers sprinkled in sections throughout. In another section there was a vegetable garden of tomatoes, collards, cabbage, and herbs. There were also apricot trees, apple trees, and lemon trees.

Often I would sit alone in Grandma's front yard and create my own dolls by picking twigs from her tree. I would carefully bend a piece back from the dark brown twig, enough to turn it until it produced a curl, and voila! I had a doll—and an imagination to make her fun to play with. By default, my doll was even brown-skin, which made her even more to my liking.

Behind Grandma's house was a small cottage that they rented out to Mr. Tony, a large, gentle, and jolly, Polynesian man. He bred Miniature Poodles. One of the brightest days of my childhood, after Daddy left, was when Mr. Tony let me pick from the litter. I chose the blackest puppy I could find, and I named her Monique.

The brightest day of my life quickly turned into one of the saddest days of my life, when my time with Monique was cut short because my mother decided to uproot us and move to the Midwest. Her friend, who was like her surrogate daughter, lived there. She was much younger than Momma, and quite a bit older than me. At least thirteen years older. By this time, I believe Momma welcomed the possibility of a new fresh start. Things were changing all around us. She had broken up with her married boyfriend and Daddy moved away to Los Angeles. The only thing that seemed to stay the same for her, was that she continued to struggle to pay the bills. So without our buy-in, Momma made the tough decision to leave California and head to a place where she believed a better life was awaiting us.

Moving to the Midwest was trouble from the beginning. My mother put Aunt Margaret in charge of shipping a lot of our stuff—memorabilia and historical stuff, including original pictures and other items, which belonged to Booker T. Washington. There was also a ring left for me by my great-aunt, Sarah Meriwether Nutter, because I was her namesake. The boxes never arrived. We lost many possessions, supposedly through the mail. My mother suspected foul play. She always wondered about the student who Aunt Margaret asked to deliver the boxes for shipping. She carried that disappointment with her all the way to her grave.

In the Midwest it was freezing in the winter months, snowy and cold. We definitely weren't used to that. I'd never been out of California before. I'd also never been in a school that had so many White students. They would all stand outside in the snow while the Black students stood huddled together indoors waiting for the first bell to ring. I believed that was more about the difference in our body temperatures, than it was about any negative racial division…perhaps it was a combination of the two.

The one plus of being in the Midwest was that we were accepted a little differently. Because we were from California, the other kids automatically thought we knew all of the Hollywood celebrities. Our peers excitedly asked if we knew the Jackson 5 and others of that era. When we told them we didn't, we were still okay. Coming from California just made us special. What a change. However, when I tried out for cheerleader, I don't think the cheerleading coach cared much about all of that because I didn't make it. Another blow to my diminished self-esteem.

When we first arrived we lived with Momma's friend and her family until we got on our feet. They lived in an upper class community, in what seemed to me to be a mansion, especially compared to where I was used to living. She had several rooms, including a library. They had a beautiful dining room where they all sat down to eat dinner together, which was something foreign to us. I am not sure why, but my brother and I ate in a small pantry where they fed their dogs. They took good care of their dogs. It was clean, but still, it was a pantry…where they fed their dogs.

At Thanksgiving dinner, on a rare occasion when we ate together, Momma's friend looked across the table and said to us, "You guys are so simple." "Simple" was a theme I added to my arsenal of words to describe who I was. These negative descriptors accumulated in my mind over several years, and remained in my psyche for a very long time.

The move turned out to be a far cry from what was promised. Momma had trouble finding work so we ended up on welfare and other government assisted programs for a short stint. That was a huge blow to whatever dignity Momma had left. Because we were low-income, we were able to secure a government subsidized home in a decent working class neighborhood, similar to the one we left in Oakland. Little did I know, it would be the last working class neighborhood we'd live in for a long time.

Momma babysat for her friend's young children more often than she cared to; especially considering she was not the babysitting type. Momma took care of her own children because she had to, but watching someone else's children was not her cup of tea. Once Momma told me, "I believe my friend may have invited us here because she needed a babysitter." She later ended up working for her friend's father who was a doctor. Her friend later told me that Momma was drinking at work; but I remember Momma's work ethic. She had a nightcap just about every night at home, but I don't believe that she would ever drink at work. Even if she did, she was so high functioning, especially at work, I doubt that it would interfere with her getting the job done.

In the short time that we lived there I have a faint memory of having an older boyfriend. He was 18-years-old, and I was just 13. I remember going places with him, and he drove, but I don't remember where or how often we'd go. We did not do much, as far as intimacy, maybe kiss. There was no sex, alcohol, or drugs. I don't remember him well, not even his name. This relationship continues to baffle me because I always felt that I was too emotionally immature, as I should have been at 13-years-old.

We lived in the Midwest for nine months, from September to June, until Momma couldn't take it anymore. That's when she decided she was worse off there than she had been in Oakland. I was the first to return to California; but this time we were going to Southern California. Momma sent me to Los Angeles to stay with her sister. She and my brother stayed in the Midwest until they could afford to join me. The plan was that we'd stay with my aunt, just until my mother landed a job and got back on her feet. Then we would find a home to rent in Los Angeles. I don't remember packing or leaving the Midwest. I just know I ended up at my aunt's house one day.

My mother's plan to move to Los Angeles changed abruptly, when one day, after I'd been there around three months, my aunt and uncle threw an extravagant party in their backyard. I was 13-years-old at the time. There were doctors, lawyers, and other high profile guests. There was a champagne fountain on the upper deck in their backyard. One of my cousin's friend's, who was around 17-years-old, kept sneaking champagne from the fountain and giving it to me. What started as innocent horseplay on his behalf, ended up with serious consequences for me. That was my first time ever having alcohol, and I quickly became intoxicated. I started yelling out the window to one of the neighbors. He was around my age, and I had a crush on him. Had I not been intoxicated, he would have never known about my feelings toward him.

I forgot a seminal rule that Momma instilled in me from a very young age. She said, "Girls should never chase boys, make the first move, or call them on the phone, unless they are returning the boy's phone call." But, on this particular day, all of that flew out the window, literally; as I yelled out my cousin's bedroom window, from the top of my lungs, to let him know just how much I liked him.

My aunt got wind that I was intoxicated. Needless to say, she was beyond upset, not to mention embarrassed by my behavior. She wrote a letter to my mother, letting her know that this arrangement may not work after all. Momma had to come up with a Plan B.

The guilt I felt for wrecking Momma's plan was overwhelming. Instead of coming to Los Angeles, my mother and brother went back to Oakland. I don't even remember packing or leaving Los Angeles, just ending up back in Oakland. After the Los Angeles incident I didn't take another drink of alcohol—at least not while I was living under my mother's roof.

Success Principle Seven—Maintaining Healthy Relationships

A favorite quote from my great-grandfather, that I constantly remind myself of, is this, "If there is any good in a person, let us seek to find it; the evil will take care of itself."

As human beings, we were created to be in relationships with one another. There are many different types of relationships: intimate, family, friendship, work, classmate, student-teacher, and employee-supervisor, to name a few. We need relationships because we are much stronger together, finding some common ground on which to stand, than we are when we are divided.

Just like in relationships with children, in all other relationships, you must be willing to meet people where they are, not where you want, or think they should be. You never know what someone is going through at any particular moment, earlier in the day, or what they have gone through in their lifetime.

Success Tips

❖ A rule of thumb is, if the good outweighs the bad, keep the relationship. If the bad outweighs the good, or even comes close, remove yourself from the relationship.

❖ Remember, no one is flawless. For every flaw we can find in someone else, they can match us one for one. Just a different flaw, most likely one they don't have themselves.

❖ Be mindful that you are not going to like everyone, and everyone is not going to like you…and that's okay.

"I believe every effort we are obliged to make to overcome obstacles will give us strength."

—Booker T. Washington

What I've Learned from my Great-Grandfather's life

No matter what I am going through in life, there will always be those who are worse off than me, and others who are doing better than I am. I can encourage those who are worse off, and be inspired by those who are doing better.

Eight

Turning 16

With misfortune piling up all around Momma, she seemed to have put her hope of having a bright future on the shelf along with her lineage…she made some bad decisions, which brought on disappointing consequences. She didn't treat me any different after the Los Angeles incident. But I felt the disappointment, and something didn't seem right. When we returned to Oakland, there was not as much communication between us as there was before. She was quite possibly depressed.

When we first returned to Oakland we moved back to our old place on 61st and Grove Street for a short while. Momma wasn't able to secure employment right away, which meant she had to sign up for welfare again. I know this stripped Momma from any dignity that she had left. She was a hard worker, and the "dignity of labor" that her grandfather instilled in former slaves, definitely spilled over to her. She absolutely enjoyed working.

In spite of my need to have encouraging, constructive communications with my mother as my closest adult role model, she never took time to encourage me or talk about her or my aspirations. I can count on one hand the number of times me and Momma went somewhere together to spend quality time. Considering her circumstances, I appreciate that she did it at all. These times gave us an opportunity to escape our reality and enjoy each other's company.

One of the earliest and most beautiful occasions that I went to with Momma was the wedding of Tramaine and Walter Hawkins. Momma was friends with Tramaine's mother, Lois, who owned a nearby restaurant when we lived in North Oakland, Lois the Pie Queen. From my recollection all of the Edwin Hawkins Singers were in the wedding party, and Tramaine and Walter sang their vows to each other. I'd never seen anything so beautiful. I also remember going to San Francisco to ride the cable cars, going to see the Nutcracker during the Christmas season, and the one that really stands out for me, is when we went to see Sammy Davis, Jr. at the Circle Star Theatre in San Carlos.

Momma loved Sammy Davis, Jr., and she wanted me to go because of a new group who was the opening act, The Sylvers. They weren't the Jackson 5, but they were cute and they held my attention with their slick dance moves, and their huge, well-groomed afros. I even enjoyed Sammy Davis, Jr., and understood why Momma was excited to see him. He was an outstanding performer, even for a young girl like me. That was a special treat. However, I can't remember how we got there because it was quite a ways from home, and Momma didn't drive. That was our last bonding experience until I was an adult and out of the house.

Another opportunity to escape my reality occurred when one of my Aunt Gloria's daughters from Los Angeles, Carolyn, moved to Oakland to attend Mills College. She stayed on campus. She invited me, at least two or three times, to spend the weekend in her dorm room with her and her roommate. It was common for them to have their classmates over. They studied, talked, laughed, listened to music, and seemingly enjoyed life. The worse thing they did, at least when I was with them, was to sneak off campus at night after their curfew to pick up a pizza from the restaurant across the street. The adventure of that was fun too. It was safe back then; but today, to do that in the same area would be insane due to a high volume of criminal activity in surrounding neighborhoods.

The whole experience was extremely positive. It planted deep in my mind that I wanted something just like that…to go to college and live on the dorms with a college roommate…after graduating from high school. After my father left he was no longer encouraging me about the importance of my education. My mother also wasn't having much discussion with me about furthering my education at this time. So, my visits with my cousin reinforced the idea my parents already planted…*education is the key to success.*

Momma soon landed a job as an office manager for Morh Housing. Maybe her fate was beginning to turn around. I'm sure one of the biggest reliefs was that she could now get off of welfare, and reclaim her dignity from the way that made her feel. Morh Housing was a brand new government housing development in West Oakland—otherwise known as "the projects." Somehow because they were new, we felt they were a step above the Acorn Housing projects across the street. However, they were both government subsidized, there was a low-income requirement, and 100% of the residents met that requirement. So, no matter how much we wanted to believe our projects were somehow better, there really was no difference. Still, it gave us a little pride to think there was. This was the first depressed neighborhood we lived in, but it wouldn't be the last… or the worst…at least not for me.

Morh Housing, like Acorn, consisted of three full blocks of mostly townhome units. In Morh Housing between the townhomes stood three high-rise apartments. We commonly referred to the different size buildings as the Low-Rises and the High-Rises. We moved to a Low-Rise unit with an upstairs and downstairs, three bedrooms, and one bath, with a small, but decent backyard. In our living room for a couch we had what appeared to be mustard yellow, pleather bus seats. I have no idea where Momma got the seats, or why she thought they would be okay for the living room. It took a while for Momma to get back on her feet.

By the time we settled in West Oakland I was entering Junior High School, which at that time consisted of the seventh, eighth, and ninth grades. Because of the environment that we lived in, there were demons all around us. Conversations about God, Jesus, church and spiritual growth were not commonly discussed in our home when I was growing up; so I had no idea how to fight these demons off.

I guess Momma still had some measure of hope for me because she was strict when it came to me going places with my friends. She only allowed me to go to certain places with certain people—and in that area of Oakland there were only a couple of families that she approved of—the Davis family from Morh Housing (Sherlyn, Eric, Bernadette, and Irvin), and the Chambers family from Acorn (Debbie, Kim, and Cathy). To this day I am still in touch with both of these families. Unfortunately, we lost Eric, Irvin, and Mrs. Chambers far too soon. But they remain in my heart forever. I have so many special memories with each of them, especially "Liz" Chambers, because she always made me feel like I was one of her own, and she went above and beyond to help me in some of my most difficult times.

Momma liked Liz, and I believe she appreciated Liz's willingness to give me what she wasn't able to at the time—a sense of nurturing. Momma was always tired after a long day's work. She would come home, fix a cocktail or two…or three, and curl up in her bed with a cigarette and a good book. As I think back, and remember her telling me this was her escape, I realize that reading must have helped her temporarily flee from where her choices landed her—a single mother raising two teenagers late in her life, with little money, and less time. She fell asleep reading, and woke up the next morning to do it all over again. Sadly, she was doing her best at that time in her life, and like so many others in her situation, she didn't realize she was setting an example for me about womanhood.

Holding on to the hope she had for us, Momma arranged for me and James to go to school out of our district. She enrolled us in Hamilton Jr. High School in East Oakland, where Aunt Margaret was the vice-principal. Momma knew that Aunt Margaret would look after us, and make sure we received the best education Hamilton had to offer.

My aunt was a smart, no-nonsense, hardworking, disciplinarian. The students either loved her or they hated her. There was no in-between. If you wanted things bad enough to work for them, she was behind you, encouraging you every step of the way. But if you were lazy and careless, needless to say, those were the students who hated her. And how they felt about her usually trickled down to the way they treated me and my brother.

Just like I wanted to disown my mother for being too light-skinned when I was in elementary school, I didn't want people to know that I was related to Aunt Margaret, but for different reasons. First, I didn't have a strong enough emotional foundation to withstand the rejection of those who hated her; and second, I was too insecure to be around the caliber of students who loved her. Both reasons were defects that would follow me for many years of my life.

While my aunt was a reinforcing presence, she was no match for the gang activity that took place at the school. The Mexican and Black students at Hamilton would fight every Friday. On a regular basis, there were helicopters flying over the school and police mulling around to stop the violence.

Momma soon had us transferred to Claremont, Jr. High in North Oakland. Claremont was somewhat better, but occasionally there were still gangs and violence, but nothing like the violence at Hamilton. The difference was that at Claremont, there were Black gangs fighting other Black gangs or just Black individuals. I was in a clique made up of the good girls, otherwise known as "squares." One of the members of our clique had a sister who was as different from her, as night is from day. Her sister was the president of the Blue Jackets gang. Because of that relationship, no one ever messed with us. The Blue Jackets had a reputation of cutting class, taking illegal substances, and fighting all the time. One day they were threatening to beat up my brother. Because I was close to the president's sister, I was able to circumvent the fight they had planned for him. My brother and I argued and fought each other all the time; but as much as we fought, I didn't want anyone else fighting him, and he didn't want anyone else fighting me.

Even with all of the brokenness in my life, I still managed to keep my grades up. Most likely it was because so many adults ingrained in me early on how smart they believed I was. So I believed it too. The few friends that I hung around with were like me; for the most part they stayed out of trouble and kept up with their studies.

At the same time, I had many acquaintances who dabbled in drugs and alcohol during and after school. My only vice at the time, other than taking a puff or two of weed when it was passed to me, was my attraction to the opposite sex…that would have an addictive pull no different than substance abuse… and it would become my downfall for many years to come.

The only thing that excited my brother more than throwing a house party, was throwing the house party and being the DJ. So, that's what he did whenever he had the opportunity, which was mostly when Momma took a turn-around trip to Reno. When I was in the ninth grade, the Jackson 5 came out with their Grammy nominated hit, "Dancing Machine." James gave a house party soon after it was first released as a single. I'm not quite sure how he pulled that off, with Momma being home that evening, but he did.

He always liked to save the best and latest music until late in the party. Around midnight he played "Dancing Machine." We all went crazy. We jumped up out of our seats, and everybody was on the dance floor, screaming "turn it up." There wasn't an idle body in the house…except Momma, who was upstairs trying to sleep. When the song ended, we headed back to our seats, or to the nearest available wall space, still highly energized. That's when James did something so cool that even I, his number one critic, couldn't shoot down—he put that song right back on…and turned it up a notch…or two. The energy was to the roof. It was a brilliant move on my brother's part. We were back on the floor, full throttle. That night he could have won the "House Party DJ of the Year" award, if there was such a thing.

However, there was one thing we overlooked in all of our excitement. One person in the house was far from feeling our passion… Momma. Before the song got going good, she stormed downstairs, snatched the plug from the wall outlet, turned on the lights, and still holding the plug in her hand, she said in no uncertain terms, "It's after midnight! The party is over, and I want everybody out of here. Now!" Embarrassment would be a gross understatement. Mortified and disgraced would be more accurate. We'd never seen Momma so mad. We all did what she said. After everyone filed out, James and I went upstairs to our perspective bedrooms, while Momma mumbled some words under her breath before going to her room and slamming the door.

Around the same time, Momma got a second job; it was part-time at the mortuary across the street from where we lived. Momma would go straight there after getting off of her full-time job, and work for about four hours Monday through Friday. She worked two jobs to make ends meet, and probably to have a break from us.

With Momma always at work, and my father gone from our lives, James and I spent a lot of time unsupervised. The older we got, the angrier we were, and the worse our fights became. We didn't realize the fights weren't about us, they were about not having any control over our circumstances—especially, our mother not being able to spend quality time with us, and our father totally abandoning us. Though he was two years my senior, and a couple inches taller than me, on some occasions I got the best of him. There was no such thing as a fair fight as far as I was concerned. I would kick, scratch, bite, and throw things. And if I was really mad, I would grab his afro and try to pull it out by the roots. Nothing was off limits, everything was fair game—lamps, dishes, chairs. If it was within my reach, it was going full force in his direction.

One day, in an effort to get away from my brother, I left the house to go visit my friend, Debbie. We were bored and decided to go visit a guy we knew in Acorn. I don't remember much about him, other than he was at least a couple years older than we were. We were in his room when he lit up a joint. That was the first time I ever smoked weed. The high hit me pretty fast, and the next thing I knew a gigantic roach crawled up his wall next to his bed. Not sure if this guy had other plans for us after he got us high in his bedroom, but I was deathly afraid of insects, and especially petrified of roaches who had an added negative effect because of their nastiness. At the first sight of the roach I jumped up and ran out of his room and through the front door like someone was after me with a gun. My friend followed. As if the roach could be anywhere near, I didn't feel safe until I was at least a block away. At that point, we laughed until we cried. Needless to say, I never went back to that guy's house again. Too bad it didn't stop me from smoking weed…a gateway that leads to other mind altering substances.

It's little wonder that subconsciously I was attracted to dysfunctional men who would meet the cycle of abuse I was used to in one form or another. There were only a few firm requirements—they had to be tall, dark, and cute…and of course…they had to have a pulse. I now know that I was vicariously trying to fix the most important relationship in my life—my derailed relationship with my father—through men who would continue to let me down. Like so many other young girls, I did this through gravitating to men who were just as emotionally unavailable as my father was when I was 11-years-old.

My first boyfriend in West Oakland lived across the street in the Acorn Housing projects. We were both in the eighth grade. He came over just about every day after school. Before Momma came home from work I would walk him to the door and we kissed good-bye. He never pressured me for more, even though our kisses were quite intense for two seventh graders. He was real cute, and had a very charming personality and a great sense of humor. I liked him a lot, so I don't know why we broke up. He was probably too nice.

When I was in the ninth grade, one evening the grandson of our former landlord in North Oakland stopped by to see me. He was at least a few years older than me, and he had a car. He was planning to go to the military when he finished high school. We sat on the couch in my living room, and he started kissing me. I tried prying his hands off, but before I knew it, I consensually lost my virginity, and it was over in all of 30 seconds. There was nothing flattering about my first time. It was easily forgettable. This is just what the both of us seemed to do. He left right after, and I don't remember hearing from him again, which was fine with me.

Why was I willing to give myself away at such a young age, so thought-lessly, and so easily? I wish I knew then what I know now—that my body is precious, and my virginity was sacred. When I think back on my father's behavior, there's no doubt that I internalized as a young girl that women were to be used as objects to satisfy a man's desires. I had no other reference to go by.

When I was 15-years-old and in the tenth grade, there was a guy I really liked. His name was Otis, but everyone called him "O-black-tis," because of his skin color…everyone except me, that is. I was attracted by his dark skin, and I liked him too much. The more he rejected me, the more I wanted him. He had really bad breath and his skin was dry and flaky. As far as I was concerned, his snide bad boy image was his best feature, and enough to make me forget all his other flaws. He'd tease me just enough to reel me in and then let me know he wasn't serious. His best demonstration of this was when he fixed me up with my first serious boyfriend. Actually he did me a favor by eliminating himself from a list of the dysfunctional relationships I would enter into. I heard he later became a preacher; but prior to that, in front of my mother, he had beat the crap out of my brother with a two by four wooden board and tore up our entire downstairs, minus the kitchen.

Prior to the fight Otis had with my brother, *Otis fixed me up with knight #1, Mario.* But it wasn't easy. Mario was in the twelfth grade. He lived less than a block away, in the Mohr Housing development with his mother and three brothers. He was after me for months before I would give in. I wasn't playing hard to get. I really didn't want to be bothered with him. He was cute enough. Tall and dark, with a wavy perm. He met the height and skin color requirement, but I think he may have been too into me for me to want him. My mother used to tell me, "All they have to do is be cute, and that's enough for you." Then she'd remind me that "it's just as easy to fall in love with a rich man as it is to fall in love with a poor man."

No matter how hard he tried, initially I wouldn't give Mario the time of day. In his many attempts to win me over, while on shoplifting sprees with his friends, he would steal things and bring them to me. I finally gave in when he shoplifted Jean Nate bath products and brought them to me. I thought, *Wow, he really likes me.* Many years later, I realized how little it took.

Mario had access to a car and during Christmas time, he took me to Piccadilly Street in East Oakland to see a chain of amazing decorations, beautifully displayed from one home to the next. I felt really special. He began to seem so cool to me. Although we were two grades apart, we had the same history class. When I was leaving class, he was going to it; and I would slip him the answers to the test we had just taken. He was smart, but he wasn't studying and instead he was hanging around the wrong crowd—students who skipped school, smoked weed, popped pills, and drank alcohol. Sometimes we would go visit his father at his apartment in East Oakland, and they sat, made small talk, and smoked weed together.

As I began to like him more and more, he was able to talk me into cutting school for the first time in my life and going to my house to hang out while my mother was at work. We started out watching television and ended up sleeping together. After a couple of times of doing this, we started skipping the television and went straight to the bed, or floor, or wherever we could make it to, in the heat of the moment. The thought of protection never crossed our minds. Fortunately it was at a time when there was a cure for just about every sexually transmitted disease. And there were none that would kill you, as long as you were treated for them.

Mario was quite a bit taller and tougher than my brother. Everyone, including my brother, knew how crazy Mario was about me. So, when I became Mario's girlfriend, James and I suddenly stopped having physical fights. In fact, the very last bout we had occurred just before I became Mario's girlfriend. I was almost sixteen and James was almost eighteen. It ended when he hauled back and socked me hard in my nose. My nose began bleeding bad. Furious and determined not to be outdone, I wiped the blood all over his clothing. Though the physical fights stopped, the verbal fights would carry us into our young adult years.

Since middle school, I had longed to be a cheerleader really bad; but I knew that privilege was reserved for the popular girls, and I was shy, reserved and quiet. When an opportunity came up to try out for homecoming cheerleader, I figured I might have a chance, so I tried out.

The day that they announced who made it I remember sitting in my seat in geometry class on pins and needles. Over the P.A. system they went down the list, and I anxiously awaited my name to be called. First they called all the seniors who made it, next all the juniors, and finally they called the sophomores; my name was the very last one to be called. By the time they got to me I was already feeling devastated as every name except mine was called. Holding back tears, I heard my name...I was ecstatic. I made it! My name was the last name on the list.

It's now sad to me how the judgment and evaluation of what others think, especially at that age, but also throughout life, can make or break us. When there is no one else at home reassuring a child of their worth—their world can fall apart in a split second.

On homecoming day in October, in my red and white uniform, representing my class, I was on top of the world. I thought, *if I could just prove myself as a homecoming cheerleader, it may lead to my getting on the regular squad...* careful not to overstep my bounds and get too close to where the real cheerleaders were.

Around that same time, after homecoming had come and gone, and many of my classmates were planning sweet sixteen birthdays...I found out that I was pregnant.

I don't recall any of the details surrounding my telling my mother that I was pregnant. I don't know how I told her... I just don't remember. I'm sure this was another instance of a traumatic incident being blocked from my memory in an effort to protect me from the pain. One thing I do know is that when I told my mother I was pregnant, she never fussed, and she never demeaned me. I'm certain I would remember the tension from that, had it occurred. I don't remember her saying I should get rid of the baby. I suppose she told my father. I don't know what my father thought...he never discussed it with me...I imagine he may have been disappointed. Still, I never got any direction from my father or mother on what to do.

Around this same time Momma had an onset of type II diabetes. I read somewhere that diabetes can be triggered by overwhelming stress, so I always felt guilty and blamed myself for her illness. With her working two jobs, and my brother and I arguing constantly, I can't imagine what this did to her. Even with all of this, one day to my surprise, she came home early from work. She came inside the house with a bag of ice cream and strawberries, which she had picked up just for me. I knew then that any shame, embarrassment, or disappointment that I caused her, was not as strong as the love that she always had for me. I believe God gives mothers keen instinct. Maybe that's how she knew that I so desperately needed that validation.

I was just a child myself. I had no idea how to raise a child, or how my life was going to change and, at the time, my mother's life as well. It never occurred to me that becoming a parent was about so much more than a 16-year-old could possibly comprehend. But that didn't matter. This baby was going to take all my pain away... or so I thought.

My mother had a coworker who was having trouble conceiving a child. She offered to adopt my unborn baby, but I refused to even entertain the idea. With my baby, I felt like I was finally going to have someone in my life who I could love, and who would reciprocate my love forever; and I believed that we'd live happily ever after. That was a tall order for anyone to take on, let alone an innocent unborn baby...especially one who wouldn't have a male role model to demonstrate for him how to love women in a healthy way. Even before I began to show, my boyfriend began to reveal his true colors.

Although I was determined that I was keeping my baby, I still carried an enormous amount of shame…the shame of having to go down to the welfare office and sign up for government assistance…and especially the shame that I'd let down and disappointed my mother. Momma was a Washington. We were Washingtons. Though Momma had long since derailed from the prominent track Booker T. Washington laid down for her, it was still in her DNA. That was something she was unable to get away from. It was inherent in her. Having to announce to her family that her 16-year-old daughter was now pregnant had to be a very degrading experience.

My sister and her husband, upon learning that I was pregnant, called me on the phone. Her husband told me how disappointed they were in me. I never knew he had hopes for me, which would actually be required in order for them to suffer a disappointment.

Around my sixth month, my mother's friend took the liberty of accompanying me to one of my prenatal appointments at the West Oakland Health Center. I can't remember how this all came about, considering I didn't know this lady well at all. After my exam she asked to speak with my doctor privately. About what, I didn't know, and I didn't ask. She spoke to him alone for a while. Afterwards he told me she asked if it was too late for me to have an abortion. I was six months pregnant at the time, and I could feel my child moving around inside of me.

I may have had other dreams for my life, but like so many youth who live in similar situations, no one was there to guide me when I most needed guidance. My mom worked two jobs to make ends meet; my father left when I was still in elementary school; I didn't get along with my brother, James; my other brother was estranged; the age difference between me and my sister was too wide for us to develop a close relationship; my oldest sister who was my father's first child, I had yet to meet; and my friends lived in environments equally, if not more dysfunctional than mine.

I felt added shame from the looks of disgust, snide remarks, and whispers that came from friends, family, and even strangers. I looked even younger than sixteen, so I would continuously rush my life away, wishing I was older so that I could look old enough to have a child.

The friends who supported me without judgment could be counted on one hand. Debbie was one of them. When we were out in public, she would carry my son and push him in his stroller, which gave me a break from the mean looks and demeaning remarks. When I had Little Mario christened, Debbie was chosen to be his godmother.

Vickie was another friend I could count on. I met her in elementary school. She was a couple of years older than me. She and my brother were friends first because they were in the same grade; but as we grew older, we became closer. She was, and still is, a rare soul, who never speaks ill about anyone. In fact, when I was around 18-years-old, I was telling her something negative about someone else, and instead of colluding with me, or wanting more details, she responded, "You talk about people too much." Her words stung, but she raised my level of consciousness that day. Although that was long ago, *the conviction stuck. I'm sure I am less critical of people than I would have been had she not checked me or been that kind of example in my life.*

Momma liked my friend Vickie, and before I became pregnant, she and I would go to parties together. She often had access to her mother's 1970s Toyota Corolla. On the weekends Vickie would pile up the small car with her closest friends and we would go to all the most popular parties. She went to high school in El Cerrito, so many of her friends were a bit more polished. However, some were more pretentious than my friends from the projects; but I loved Vickie, so I tolerated her friends. She continued to take me with her when I became pregnant, even when I started to show. On my own, and out of shame and embarrassment, when I could no longer button my pants I stopped going out with them. Once I gave birth, Vickie's mother would often babysit so that I could live that part of my youth out. Like her daughter, she didn't judge me either.

As I began to show, I transferred from my high school to a school in East Oakland. It was a small classroom setting, located within an elementary school with a large room reserved for pregnant teenagers. There was only a handful of students. Not that teenage pregnancy rates were uncommon in the seventies, but many gave up on their educations and dropped out, deciding to trade in school for full-time parenting. Other students stayed in their traditional high school, and some had abortions or miscarriages. Whatever the reason, I am proud to say that my new classmates and I were committed to staying in school. We were all in the same predicament, so we weren't judging one another. We received lots of individual attention from the instructors. I was able to concentrate on my work there, instead of wondering what everyone was thinking and saying about me. Thus, I was able to earn excellent grades.

In 1975 Earth Wind and Fire, the former little known band that I used to watch practice in one of the parents of a member's home, was taking the country by storm. They were no longer the opening act, they were now the show. While my cousin's boyfriend was no longer part of the band, I was still in awe that I got to see them up close and personal before they became famous. When I was around six months pregnant my boyfriend came over and boastfully showed me two tickets that he had bought for an Earth Wind and Fire concert that was coming to the Oakland Coliseum.

Initially I was excited because I automatically thought the tickets were for the two of us. It wasn't like he was trying to hide them. He whipped them out right in front of me. *Even he couldn't be that mean...could he?* Within five minutes of showing me the tickets, he announced that the second ticket was not for me. It was for another female; not just any female, but one who happened to be the sister of one of my friends. Barely sixteen and pregnant, though this was undoubtedly bad enough, my boyfriend's callous display of deceit was just one of the many heartaches I'd suffer in this relationship.

Believing it would make me feel better, a couple of my closest friends insisted that I go with them to the concert. Reluctantly I agreed to go. Amongst the enormous crowd in the Oakland Coliseum, in the dark, I spent the evening looking for my boy-friend, feeling miserable, and quietly crying through the entire concert. From that point on, he continued to degrade me in one form or another, mostly with other women. Over the next three years, two weeks rarely went by without us breaking up and getting back together again. By taking him back, I was actually helping him to be who he was. I was validating that what my boyfriend was doing to me was okay. It took a long time for me to realize that I had the "power" all along.

My boyfriend was best friends with the brother of one of my close girlfriends, Sherlyn. She saw a lot, and told me everything she saw him doing with other girls. After she told me, she would say, "But you can't tell him that you know." I used to wonder, "What good was it for me to know, and not be able to do anything about it." It was pointless. Her reports hurt me bad. Although I would agree to not say anything to him, I knew keeping silent was not an option. I couldn't wait for her to leave so that I could get to him. Every single time I went ballistic.

Like my parents, we went back and forth, not just attacking, but assassinating one another's character. It wasn't easy trying to fix my relationship with my father through this relationship. But because I was unconscious that that was what I was doing, it would go on for far too long. The worst part was that this emotional and verbal abuse would continue once our innocent child was born. But who cared? After all, we were selfishly trying to get our needs met. That's how generational cycles of abuse continue to spiral down. It was carried down from my parents, and now I was unknowingly getting ready to carry it down to my child.

In my ninth month, I had false labor. My baby's father was nowhere to be found, so Aunt Margaret took me and my mother to the hospital. They sent me home and the next day I went into labor, for real. Mario came to the hospital this time, but he didn't stay. My mother stayed with me the whole time. I was in labor for 18 hours, and Momma drank about 10 cups of coffee so that she would not fall asleep.

I was calm until the nurse told me I was not dilated enough and the doctor would have to perform a Caesarean section. I nearly lost it. The pains got worse as I tensed up. I was so frightened, just a child myself, in so much pain, with an IV, a catheter, and an enema. But Momma stayed calm, and that helped me to calm down.

Finally I gave birth to a seven-pound, thirteen-ounce baby boy. When the nurse came into the room to bring him for the first time, she had two babies in her arms. I wondered which one was mine. In my head I was saying, "Eenie, meanie, minie, moe…" and trying to figure out which one was the cutest, hoping to get that one. Once she brought my baby to me, I held him close, laid him on my chest and we both instantly fell into a deep peaceful sleep. For me, it was a sleep that was long overdue. Each time the nurse would bring him to me for the five days I stayed in the hospital, I'd hold him and we'd fall asleep. Many studies indicate that babies can feel tension between their parents even in the womb. If this is true, it's no wonder he was tired.

After I delivered Little Mario, I returned to my traditional high school. Across the street there was a daycare for the babies of students. On one hand that was a blessing. On the other hand…what did it say about teenage pregnancy and parenting within our community?

Always one to seek self-improvement, I attended a workshop in East Oakland for single teenage mothers. The only one of its kind, the workshop provided resources and encouragement for beating the odds. It was facilitated by Dezi Woods-Jones. I felt forever indebted to Dezi for her inspiration. As God would have it, our paths crossed many years later as members of the same church, Allen Temple in Oakland. When I saw her there I was able to express my gratitude to her...again. Later I found out she was good friends with my first cousin, Congresswoman Diane Watson; I then believed our paths were always destined to cross.

My son, Mario, was born on September 16. Ironically, I turned 16-years-old on February 16, of that same year. It would seem like the number 16 should have represented life for me, but instead it represented enormous amounts of shame and guilt that I would carry for a long time.

Success Principle Eight—Personal Responsibility

When we blame a group, an individual, or a situation for our circumstances, we strip ourselves of our power to move beyond the circumstance. We become victimized and weak when we give our power over to someone else.

On the other hand, when we take personal responsibility for where we are, and where we want to be, we empower ourselves in a way that nothing else can; and from that point, there is nothing that can stand in the way of our progress.

Of course, there are always instances when we may have to depend on others, and situations are simply out of our control. But even in the most challenging situations we can take personal responsibility to find the silver lining.

Success Tips

❖ Taking personal responsibility for where our choices landed us is empowering.

❖ Blaming someone else for our circumstances will keep us stuck in them.

❖ It's self-deprecating to expect the same people we blame for our adverse situations, to be the very people we expect to get us out of them.

"We should not permit our grievances to overshadow our opportunity."

—Booker T. Washington

What I've Learned from my Great-Grandfather's life

If I tell a child or a struggling adult that they can make it, they will have a much better chance, than they will if I tell them they are doomed to fail.

Nine

Tassafaronga Village

After I got home from the hospital with my baby, my relationship with his father continued on the decline. There was never any real excitement from him about our newborn son. Our fights only escalated. It seemed that after Little Mario was born we would break up and then make up at least once a week over the entire time that we were together.

After my son's father graduated from high school he went to a vocational school, the East Bay Skills Center. On the upside, he studied drafting there, and when he completed the program he began working contract jobs for large corporations, including Pacific Gas and Electric Company, and Pacific Bell. On the downside, he met a girl at the Skills Center who he began going out with, and he started what would become a long stint of cheating with other women.

When the girl from the Skills Center got wind somehow that he had a girlfriend and a son, she left him alone. I suppose she had a level of decency and self-worth that the others who came along after her didn't have. As he continued getting high with his friends, his goals began to change from being a responsible working man, to becoming a drug dealer, and a pimp with lots of women.

Most of our fights were about other women and Little Mario's needs. I remember once when I asked him for money for diapers, and he told me he was saving his money to get a coat out of the layaway. When he finally got it out, he came over to show it off. It was a full length navy blue coat, with real white fur around the collar. It was made up of alternating leather and suede diamonds which were about an inch in diameter, stitched together to make up the coat. I wasn't impressed at all. In fact, I was hurt. This behavior played out over and over, just a different material item each time. I thought I could change him back to the person he was in the beginning. It took four long, miserable, degrading years to convince myself that I couldn't.

My mother was sick and tired of the madness of our home environment, and my brother's total disregard for me or her. In addition to her recent diagnosis of type II diabetes, our bickering and constant fighting, and no one ever cleaning up downstairs, became too much for her to bear. To top it off, now there was a baby added to the mix.

Before Little Mario turned one-year-old, my mother left us to fend for ourselves. She moved up the street to a one-bedroom unit in one of the three high-rise apartment buildings. Her office was in the same building. I don't remember her ever packing, or leaving for that matter…I just know that one day she was gone. When Momma left, I rarely came out of my upstairs bedroom. When I did come downstairs, it was only to leave out the front door, which was adjacent to the bottom of the steps, so I could go out without going into the living room or kitchen.

By this time I was 17-years-old, and James was now 19-years-old. He couldn't stand me, and the feeling was mutual…I couldn't stand him either. Very soon after Momma moved, James left too. He moved in with a friend and his family across the street in the Acorns. I was living there alone with my son.

Though Mario and I still considered ourselves a couple, his visits were becoming few and far between. I never liked being alone... partly because I was afraid, and partly because I was lonely. Little Mario's company helped with the latter part. I was also very squeamish when it came to any kind of flesh wound or medical emergency, and I couldn't handle spiders, or anything crawling, with the exception of my child. Before I could just scream and Momma or James would come. Or if someone else happened to be around, they would deal with the situation. When Little Mario hurt himself up to that point, there was always someone else around us to examine the damage. They would let me know it was alright for me to look, because he was going to be okay, and I could stop freaking out.

Little Mario was a boy's boy from the minute he began to sit up by himself. He liked to take risks, and he had more than his fair share of accidents for someone his age. That hasn't changed—as he recently bought a Harley, his toys just got bigger.

One evening when he was around one-year-old, while we were home alone, I turned my back for two seconds. That's when he decided to push a tiny metal bolt screw all the way up his nose. When I turned around and saw him starting to do it, I yelled, "You better not!" I guess the curiosity of what would happen overruled my threat, because he kept on with his plan. I darted toward him as quickly as I could. When he saw me coming, he hurried and completed his act. By the time I got to him, he had finished pushing it as far as he could get it up there. Then he started crying. Frantic, among other curse words, I yelled, "What the *hell* am I going to do?!"

There was no one around to help me, and I knew the screw had to be removed. *It's funny how the skills we never thought we have, immediately kick in, and become second nature in times of trouble.* I can't remember exactly how I removed it without pushing it farther up his nose. I do remember it being a difficult task, where precision was of utmost importance. It seems it was the tweezers that finally worked. I also remember it taking quite some time, and several attempts before I got it out. I was pretty proud of myself when it was all over. Luckily the screw was flat at the end, and there was no blood. My motto for myself and others, from that day forward was, "You can do anything you put your mind to." Anything!

After Mario was born, I purchased a compact refrigerator to keep in my room, so that I didn't have to go up and down the stairs in the middle of the night when he needed his formula. With the refrigerator there in my room, I was able to avoid the kitchen. But one day, for some reason, I decided to go in there. I was already afraid of what I might see, because no one bothered cleaning up when my mother and brother were there, and they'd been gone for at least a week. I was disgusted by the maggots I saw crawling on the exposed part of a sausage link that was left in a pot of greasy water on the stove. I screamed and ran out of there as fast as I could—as if the maggots were chasing me. Unlike the screw in my son's nose, there was no way I was willing to brave that one. I knew then I had to find somewhere else to live right away. Without a doubt, our unhealthy environment was unfit for Mario.

At the time, I was receiving welfare and food stamps. I also received a monthly check from Social Security because my father turned 65-years-old when I was still in high school. The welfare and food stamps propelled me to do better because I was so humiliated and embarrassed to have to live on them. The food stamps were especially hard because they presented a public embarrassment. Whenever I was in the line in the grocery store, I would glance at the people behind me. If they appeared to have a job, I would get out of line so they would not see that I was paying for my groceries with food stamps. The Social Security money was an added incentive to stay in school.

On some level, I guess I knew I was a Washington, and that my great-grandfather did not work tirelessly so that former slaves and their children, let alone his own direct descendants, would end up dependent on government assistance. Some uninformed people today have it wrong. They think my great-grandfather simply wanted us to be workers just like we were as slaves. But that is very far from the truth. Instead he intended for us to become business, land, and property owners. He believed to do this, we needed to play to our strengths, and become aware of the latest developments in those areas, and then to become superb at what we already knew. Countless financially secure former slaves, and their descendants, were the manifestation of his advice. In fact, the book, "Christian Business Legends," cited that by 1905, Tuskegee, the school my great-grandfather opened in 1881, produced more self-made millionaires than Harvard, Yale, and Princeton combined.

Little Mario's fraternal grandmother, Sarah, worked for the Oakland housing authority. While she did what she could to help me find a decent place, Little Mario and I were able to stay a while with her niece, Jackie. They were both godsends. They were neutral, fair, and supportive. I spent a lot of time with Sarah and her sister, Jackie's mother, Ola. They took me everywhere with them. They cared about me, and wanted the best for me. They constantly urged me to leave the relationship. His mother would always say, "I love my son, but wrong is wrong." She was no stranger to my situation, as she raised her four boys on her own. She also offered to raise Little Mario several times, but I continuously turned her down. I gave birth to him, and I was determined that I could raise him, with or without his father. Besides, he was going to be my golden boy, the little man who would finally bring me eternal bliss...

It wasn't long before Sarah provided me with three different addresses from the Housing Authority to take a look at. They were all in East Oakland. The first place I visited was a freshly painted unit in the 69th Village housing projects. The second was a unit in a newly renovated apartment building around 90th and MacArthur. The last place was a brand new, from the ground up, four unit building that sat in the middle of four older two story apartment buildings in the 85th Village projects, also known as Tassafaronga Village. They were all in some of the roughest neighborhoods in Oakland, especially for a 17-year-old single mother. Today they are commonly referred to as the "killing fields."

Out of the three, the brand new building in Tassafaronga was the most appealing. I would be the first tenant, and it kind of gave me the feeling of having a fresh start. At 17-years-old, I had my first place. I was on my own, raising my son alone…with the exception of the times his father would stay there, between breakups and being between the legs of other girls. Because it was a government sub-sidized property, his name could not be on the tenant agreement. So, he conveniently used the fact that his name was not on the rental agreement as his excuse to stay away whenever it suited him.

There's no doubt in my mind, that if that excuse was not available, he would have come up with something else. That's why, contrary to popular belief, I don't believe the welfare system had as much to do with the break-down of Black families as has been portrayed.

I do think, like with my son's father, it was mostly a convenient excuse, which leads to another pet peeve:

> *Only when we take personal responsibility for our issues, will we have the power to change them. In other words, whether we are referring to a married couple blaming the other spouse, a classroom full of students blaming the instructor, or an entire race of people blaming a system or another race of people, as long as we place the blame outside of ourselves, we strip ourselves of the power to do anything about it, and place it into the hands of someone we claim is purposely harming us.*

Thus, why would anyone want, expect, or trust someone like that to help them? The power lies within, but only if we believe that it does.

My mother visited me a couple of times in Tassafaronga Village. I don't remember much about our visits except, she fell in love with Little Mario after he was born, and it also seemed like she felt obligated to come. Although she lived in a government housing development in West Oakland at the time, there was something about her being in this neck of the woods that seemed so far out of place for her. I was always anxious for her to leave before it got dark because once the sun went down, it got dangerous. She didn't drive so she would have to walk several blocks to catch a bus that took her to downtown Oakland where she'd transfer to the bus line that dropped her off right in front of her apartment building. I worried about her until she arrived home. Momma was the same about me. Even when I was well into my adult years, if she knew I was out at night, or in bad weather, she would call to make sure I arrived home safely.

Little Mario has always been smart, well beyond his years. He began walking at just nine-months-old. I don't think I have ever been more excited than when he took his first steps. We were still living in West Oakland, and we were outside with my good friend, Sherlyn, who was sometimes known as a prankster, having gotten it honestly from her two older brothers, Eric and Irvin. Sherlyn somehow got the notion that she was going to see if she could teach Little Mario how to walk. She would take him a few steps away from me, stand him up, turn him around so that he was facing me, and then she'd let him go. He always got up without crying, and with his daredevil spirit, he went back for more. So, despite my uneasiness, I didn't interfere. After falling the first few times, he finally took off walking. I was thrilled to death. Apparently Sherlyn and Little Mario could see something in him that I couldn't see at the time. On that particular day, there was actually a method to Sherlyn's madness. I was grateful to her, and so proud of my son. With all the negativity going on around me, the inspiration I received from that, was much needed.

For Little Mario's father, his walking so soon came with a high price. He was about thirteen months old when I moved to Tassafaronga. Because he could walk pretty well by then, his father felt like he should be able to go to the bathroom on his own too. Therefore, he decided to potty train him. He used his own "death by fire" method to train him. He began by putting him in underwear. Whenever he didn't make it to the bathroom on time, he then spanked him relentlessly. I couldn't stand it; but because his father was selling drugs, and he was his own best customer, there was no limit to what he might have done if I interfered. After two weeks, Little Mario was completely potty trained.

Our verbal fights soon escalated from character assassinations to physical abuse. And unlike the fights I grew up having with my brother, I never won any with my son's father. He was much taller than I was, and the drugs only exasperated his anger. Adding insult to injury, there were no secrets in Tassafaronga Village. I'm sure everything that went on behind the closed doors of my unit, was heard by my neighbors. When they held a private conversation in their living room, I felt like an unseen guest. Even whispers traveled right through the paper thin walls. The phrase "personal business" didn't exist there.

There were three sisters across the street in one of the four sur-rounding apartment buildings. They were all very pretty, and they appeared to be too sophisticated to live in that environment. Unlike many of the tenants, they were always well-groomed and well-dressed. They were all close to my age, and like me, they were all in high school. The odds that they would finish high school were better than mine because they didn't have any children, and although their mother appeared to have some type of a mental illness, they lived with her. Hence, they didn't have to change diapers and pay bills. Their mother's illness may have been schizophrenia. In the middle of the night I remember always hearing loud screams, which sounded like it may have been coming from the cats they owned. I never found out what was going on up there.

Although, from outward appearances it seemed as if I might have a lot in common with the three of them, it took a while for them to warm up to me. When they saw me they would look me up and down, and cut their eyes at me. Later I found out why they did this. I remember one of them saying to me, "I used to think you were a bitch until we were passing each other on the sidewalk and you smiled at me...and your smile was so friendly that it changed my mind about you." After they warmed up to me, they were amazed to learn that I didn't live with a parent.

The entire housing development was much smaller in size and population than the projects I came from in West Oakland—yet, I witnessed a lot worse activity, in much closer range, on a more frequent basis. Gun shots, domestic abuse, child abuse, violent crimes, con games, drug deals and substance abuse were commonplace in Tassafaronga Village. With the exception of the gun shots, each one of these activities took place at least once behind the doors of my own unit; and the one exception took place close by.

I witnessed one of my neighbors who I'd come to really like, die on a gurney before he made it inside the ambulance. He was very friendly and respectful. Everyone liked him. He never gave anyone a reason not to. He was always smiling. He would never walk by without speaking and asking how I was doing. He mostly kept to himself and minded his own business. Occasionally he stopped by my unit to see if I had anything of value that he could sell, or if I wanted to buy anything someone else had given him to sell. Usually it was clothes, jewelry, or small used, sometimes broken, appliances. I never bought anything, but I would save Little Mario's clothes that were getting too small for him. They were always bagged up, waiting for his inevitable knock at my door. I thought he used the money for food, but later found out he was a heroin addict.

The sound of sirens were common in Tassafaronga, to the point that it just seemed like a normal occurrence. But on one particular afternoon when the EMT showed up at his door, everyone around seemed to take notice. The crowd of concerned neighbors grew larger. Everyone stood around, until the EMT, in a loud voice shouted, "Clear!" before putting the defibrillator on my neighbor's chest. They tried over and over to revive him. When the defibrillator didn't start him breathing again, they began CPR, but to no avail. I hoped for my friend to breathe again, but instead I watched him die. That experience taught me never to judge a drug addict. You never know how someone might decide to medicate their pain, or how they may try to escape from their reality.

When my son's father was away he'd leave marijuana in the house for me to sell if someone happened to come over to buy weed. Although he never gave me any of the profit, he expected me to make sure he didn't lose a sale. One evening two of his cousins, knowing he was not there, came by and easily swindled me out of a couple of packages. He was furious with me for being so naïve. But selling drugs was not on my list of the things I wanted to excel at.

During the time that I lived there, we became really good friends with another couple in Tassafaronga, Grace and Trey. She was a year or two older than me, and Trey was a couple of years older than my son's father. Grace was a petite 5'1", and weighed about 90 pounds soaking wet. She was very cute, with caramel-colored skin, and short red hair that she usually wore in a nice buzz cut. She had a high pitch laugh that sometimes echoed through the thin project walls like symphony notes. She was also very feisty, with a short fuse, mostly toward Trey. Although Momma didn't care for Grace from the first time she met her, you might say that Grace was to me, what Uncle Effie was to her. Like Uncle Effie, when it came to Grace, you couldn't let her small frame fool you. She also owned a loaded gun that she wasn't afraid to use if she had to…and she did.

Trey was a huge 6'6" giant of a man, the size of an NFL linebacker. They had a son who was about one year older than Little Mario. Grace was only 14-years-old when her son was born, and Trey was 16-years-old. The six of us became really close.

When we all first met, Trey immediately took a liking to us. He deemed himself our protector, which was good because everyone was afraid of him. He had weapons that he wasn't afraid to use if someone tried to get over on him. Trey could be counted on to step in between me and any predators. I needed a protector; I was a young girl with a baby, and we were alone a lot. I weighed all of 120 pounds. What could I do in a neighborhood riddled with drugs, guns, and criminal activity?

Grace and I had to feel each other out before letting our guards down long enough to enter into each other's space. Eventually we became good friends. In some ways we were the same—we were both on welfare; we both lived in the projects; we were both teenage mothers; we were both in dysfunctional relationships with our sons' fathers, who lived with us when it was convenient for them; we were both very sweet unless you gave us a reason to be otherwise, in which case we were known to fly off the handle; and we were both unpretentious. That was enough for us to be supportive and accepting of each other, and meet each other's criteria for a friendship.

Still, in many ways, we were different. She never ventured outside of the poverty-stricken environment she grew up in. I lived in working class neighborhoods and often visited my well-to-do relatives until I was 13-years-old. She wasn't ashamed about being on welfare, and I was humiliated by it. Grace dropped out of school before her son was born. I was struggling through high school when I met her. Grace had a shorter fuse than I did, and you never knew when she was going to blow up. It could take a lot before I would finally explode.

Trey and my son's father had a lot in common. They both had super big egos. They were tall, with nice dark complexions, and "bad-boy" images that seemed to magnetically draw other women to them. Some of the girls they had on the side lived right there among us in Tassafaronga. They were both emotionally and physically abusive. And they both sold and abused their own inventory of illegal drugs. Like my son's father, he was his own best customer.

Grace and Trey used heroin to escape their emotional pain. Until I met them and our other neighbor who overdosed from heroin, I never knew anyone who used heroin. For that matter, I never saw anyone do anything other than drink alcohol and smoke marijuana. But that all changed when I got to Tassafaronga. Maybe Trey introduced heroin to Grace…I don't know. I never asked her.

Trey's vicious addiction did not allow him to remain employed for any significant length of time. When he did work, he brought in good money. He worked down at the shipyard, but the work was sporadic. In between calls he sold drugs.

On his better days, Trey was the friendly, gregarious type who could tell an off the cuff joke, or make a spontaneous remark that would have us laughing until we cried. On his worse days you might see Trey stooped over in a narcotic nod. At other times he could be mean, and he had a violent temper, especially towards Grace. The transformation came when the Union wasn't calling Trey to come down to the shipyard, or when he didn't have money to buy drugs to sell, or when Grace's monthly welfare check was depleted and there was nothing left to feed their son or their addiction. On those days, it was almost certain that Grace would get beaten up by Trey.

The day finally came when Trey pushed Grace over the edge. I could hear her screaming and cussing at Trey from the top of her lungs. I ran to the front window to see what was going on. That night I witnessed my friend chasing her physically abusive boyfriend through the complex until she caught up to him, and then I heard a gun go off. I don't think Trey realized that God was on his side that night. In her rage, I believe she would have killed him; but lucky for both of them, Trey was over a foot taller than her. Between that and her not being a match for the power of the gun, the bullet only hit him in his upper leg.

Eventually Trey ended up in prison where his leg was amputated when he was stabbed several times during a fight. Years later their son ended up in prison for aiding and abetting a murder. Grace ended up having three other children by two other men, and remaining on welfare. The projects of East Oakland were hell. I knew that without a doubt, somehow I had to get out of there. I had so many things to worry about. My money was always running low. Sometimes I didn't know how I was going to pay the PG&E, or how I was going to make it to school for the rest of the week. I laid there in silence, fixated on the images I'd seen earlier in the evening…wishing another day of my life away.

While living in Tassafaronga, when I turned eighteen I'd heard about a modeling agency that was about a twenty minute bus ride away. I was interested in learning how to model. I thought that might help me with my confidence. When I arrived there, I found it to be a hole in the wall. The room was set up like a classroom, and there were several other young ladies sitting in the folding chairs and waiting to see what this place had to offer. The owner of the agency was an older male, possibly in his fifties, who was also a professional photographer. He took individual pictures of us, as we walked and posed. It didn't appear that he, or any of us, knew what we were doing. That dream was cut short when the owner called me at home and invited me to go out on a date. I agreed over the phone just to get rid of him, but I never returned to his modeling agency again…or any other modeling agency for that matter.

Back in the "real world," in addition to stealing my welfare money to buy drugs, my son's father was cheating on me with a girl who lived in the apartment building across the street from my unit. She was all of five feet tall, and she had an identical twin sister. They were petite, and they had nice shapes, but their clothes were usually disheveled, and their hair was always a mess. Describing them as "rough around the edges" is an understatement.

One evening, she and her entourage of about eight other girls came knocking on my door. When I opened the door, they walked into my house as if I'd invited them in. Her purpose for coming was to let me know she was seeing my boyfriend, who of course, was not there. She didn't say it in any mean or vindictive sort of way. In fact, it was almost as if she was making normal conversation to see how I'd react. Her friends seemed more dangerous than she did. I was afraid, but fortunately that evening I had a few of my own friends over…who were also afraid, and no match for these girls, but they were there nevertheless.

One of her friends, who was not as composed as she was, brushed me slightly with a lit cigarette. I wasn't sure if it was an accident, but I somehow doubted that it was. I had no idea what their full intentions were, and I was trying hard not to provoke them. Somehow it seemed that the girl had somewhat of a conscience and although she could have instructed her posse to jump on me, she kept them under control. The worse thing she did was inform me that she and my boyfriend had sex earlier that day. Then, still composed, she went on to say, "When we were done, we watched you out of my bedroom window walking across the street to the store." She didn't say why they were watching me, how long they were watching me, or what they were saying as they watched me. And I didn't ask. But it hurt just to know that they were. I felt like I'd been stabbed in the heart with a jagged edged knife. As I stood there stunned that she was in my house, telling me these things, my heart was bleeding. I fought back tears, while not saying a word. After about a good ten minutes, they all filed out of my place, leaving only a small cigarette burn on my arm…and an open wound in my heart. The rest of that evening is a blur.

My son's father and I continued our weekly ritual of breaking up and making up. He began integrating more serious drugs into his drug use—mainly cigarettes laced with PCP, aka Angel Dust. For a minute I joined him, believing it might take the edge off the misery I felt. But I was wrong. Angel Dust was much more serious than that. It could be lethal. Only by the grace of God was I able to put it down cold turkey after a whole week of smoking it every day. Unfortunately, my son's father didn't receive the same grace as I did. He continued smoking for a long time to come.

A lot was going on then, especially during the time we were smoking Angel Dust. A lot of people were in and out of my house, partying day and night—throughout the week. As my environment would inevitably indicate in my weakness, I fell prey to experimenting with several other different substances at least once, including Mescaline and Freebase. The only form of use I did not experiment with, thank God, was intravenous use. A combination of the fear of needles and the fear of hard physical addiction was much stronger than my desire to take away my pain.

All during this time, my son and Grace's son were in our midst. They were unaware of the self-destruction taking place among their parents, just a few yards away from where they were playing with their toys. They were both under four-years-old at the time. When I think about it, I still shake my head, wondering, "What was I thinking?" I guess that was the problem…I wasn't thinking.

In a violent drug induced rage, following a verbal argument about something I've since forgotten, my son's father pushed me down hard on the floor. I landed on a sharp metal object that tore through my pants and cut me in between my vaginal area, causing me to bleed. Afraid of what was coming next, I got up and ran out of the house, leaving everything behind, including Little Mario. I looked behind me as I ran across the grass field behind my unit, and Little Mario was running behind me with my wallet in his tiny little hands. I stopped to wait for him, and when he caught up to me he held his arms up for me to take him with me. I scooped him up. We held tightly to each other as we hurried up 85th Avenue until we reached the bus stop on East 14th Street. We headed for my mother's apartment in West Oakland.

Momma made a strategic move when she first left me and James in Morh Housing. She moved into a one bedroom unit. She didn't have enough room for anyone else besides herself. Besides that, her rental agreement did not allow guests to stay over a certain amount of days. Her day job involved making sure the rest of the tenants followed the rules, so she certainly would not violate them herself. If my mother was one thing, she was a highly moral and ethical employee. She used to gasp at the thought of me taking personal calls at work, or calling in sick, especially on a Monday, Friday, or the day before or after a holiday. For her, that was unheard of.

Momma didn't know anything about how bad things were going for me in Tassafaronga Village. If she did, she didn't let on, perhaps in an attempt to protect her own heart. Needless to say, after a day, I went back to my place. As is common in the cycle of abuse in domestic violence relationships, I let Little Mario's father talk his way back into my life, still convinced I could change him.

Through it all, during the school months I managed to get up every morning to get myself and Little Mario dressed, fed, and off to school. Taking the walk to East 14th Street to catch the first of two buses with a baby in the winter months was not an easy task. We would then transfer downtown Oakland. After getting off the second bus, I would rush to get Little Mario to daycare and then get myself to class. Against all odds, and defying the statistics, I am proud to say that I had the grades and more than enough credits to finish high school in January—six months ahead of the rest of my class. It was a great day when I completed school, and I didn't have to get up, get ready, catch the bus, get Mario to day care, and get to class any longer.

Six months later, I returned to walk the stage with my classmates. Sitting on the field among all of the other graduates at Oakland Technical High School, waiting for my name to be called, was one of the most uplifting moments in my life. My friend Sherlyn was sitting next to me. Momma was really proud of me. This was one of the best days in my life…my first real sense of accomplishment.

Later in life I would learn that at 15-years-old, my great-grandfather, Booker T. Washington, traveled nearly 500 miles, mostly by foot, to get his formal education from Hampton Institute, today known as Hampton University. He graduated three years later with honors. Unbeknownst to me at the time, I had that same blood running through my veins.

Success Principle Nine—Achieving Excellence

Excellence is the culmination of setting forth your highest qualities. For me that includes, perseverance, determination, and will. It may sound overwhelming, but it definitely is not. We are not born with excellence, but we are born to become excellent.

Excellence is not perfection. It is an attitude. We can still fail and be excellent. It's our internalized attitude that makes us excellent. It's the way we look at the world, and what we do in the world that makes us excellent. Mistakes are seeds for improvement.

An effective strategy for achieving excellence is by learning from not just your mistakes, but learning from the mistakes of others. Contrary to popular belief, personal experience is not always the best way to learn a lesson. In fact, it's much easier on us if we avoid the traps we see others fall into.

Success Tips

❖ If we take little steps along the way, on a daily basis, with excellence as our goal, we become excellent.

❖ As we rid ourselves of the need to be perfect, and just do our very best each day, we become excellent.

❖ If our attitude becomes one of harvest instead of one of bareness, we become excellent.

❖ Even when something appears insignificant, when we approach it with excellence, we become excellent.

Sarah Washington O'Neal Beating the Odds

Sarah's 1977 Graduation Picture

Little Mario (1979)

Sarah, Little Mario, and Regarah (1981)

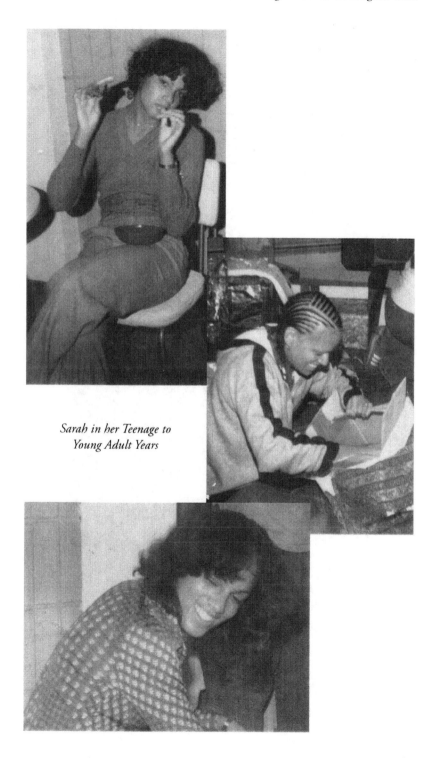

*Sarah in her Teenage to
Young Adult Years*

Sarah in Her Young Adult Years

Sarah and her Mother enjoying time together in Las Vegas

"Let us hold up our heads, and with firm and steady tread go manfully forward. No one likes to feel that he is continually following a funeral procession."

—Booker T. Washington

What I've Learned from my Great-Grandfather's life

I choose to see the opportunity instead of the adversity. Whether in a family meeting, a classroom, or a board room, it is more favorable for my cause, if I come from a spirit of altruism, than if I come from a spirit of bitterness, anger, and/or entitlement.

Ten
Two Steps Forward, One Step Back

When I was 19-years-old and my brother was 21, he moved from West Oakland to live with my father in a small apartment in Los Angeles—where they mentally and emotionally abused each other. My father was no longer working. He was still a heavy drinker, and was probably drunk most of the time. Nevertheless, my brother invaded his space. Besides that, my brother apparently didn't understand that trying to reason with a drunk is unreasonable.

Soon after graduating from high school, my mother was able to get me in an apartment in one of the high-rise buildings, where she worked in West Oakland. It was just a block away from where she lived. My good friend's mother, Liz, came to Tassafaronga in a pickup truck, and she helped me move everything. I think we got it all in one trip. Thank God, I was out of there!

Things were beginning to look up; but it would still be quite a climb to get to where I aspired to be—off of all government assistance, a college graduate, with a decent job, making a comfortable living. I often daydreamed about how nice that would feel. By this time, my son's father and I were seeing less and less of each other, as he continued doing more and more drugs, and of course, seeing other women.

After high school, I worked for a little while at the Jack London Inn Hotel doing office work, while attending the College of Alameda, a local community college. With the added responsibilities of taking care of my son, and making sure the bills were paid, it took me twice as long to finish college. Still, I didn't stop until I received my associate of arts degree in business management. Again, Momma was proud of me.

I think that one of the reasons Momma was always so proud of me was because she was unable to give me all the things she wanted me to have, and despite that, I kept accomplishing important and meaningful goals on my own. I was a high achiever, making things happen for myself, without her having to exert much energy.

Grace and I reconnected for a short stint a couple of times after I moved out of Tassafaronga Village. Once was when she talked me into cashing a $150.00 money order that was mistakenly delivered to her address. The original payee's name was close enough to her name for her to easily change it. Because she had no I.D. or bank account at the time, I let her sign it over to me. I deposited it in my checking account and we split the money.

We thought we got away clean until I received a certified letter from the U.S. Postal Inspection Service months later, regarding the money order. They easily traced it back to me because of my I.D. and my bank account. Frightened to death, I went to the main

Post Office in West Oakland, as instructed in the letter. When I got off the elevator, I was escorted to an office where two serious looking men were waiting for me.

One sat behind a desk, and the other sat in a chair off to his side. They gestured for me to take a seat. With the exception of having a Caesarean section when I delivered my son, I was more nervous than I've ever been in my entire life. Until I reached the office of the postal investigators, I had no idea of the serious nature of what I'd done. These were criminal investigators. The first thing they did was recite my Miranda rights. That's when I knew I was in real trouble. I wanted to cry and die at the same time. This was even more serious than I'd first imagined. They asked questions, I told the truth. I'd never been in any trouble like that before.

Hoping the investigators were judging a book by its cover, I sat there nervously, trying to portray an angelic-like demeanor that exuded innocence. It seemed to have worked. They let me go with just a slap on the wrist, and a harsh warning about what would happen if there was a repeat offense. I just had to pay the entire amount back within a short timeframe. There would not even be a record of the unlawful deed, as long as I paid the money back on time. I was so thankful. When we were wrapping up the meeting, as I tend to do when I am nervous and grateful at the same time, I uncharacteristically started running off at the mouth…talking about how something similar but not illegal happened to me on another occasion. My internal voice told me to, "Shut up!" When I was away from the office, I said to myself, *What were you thinking, Sarah? You were about to talk yourself right back into trouble.* Under those circumstances, less is definitely more.

I still wasn't out of the woods yet, because I was flat broke, and the payment was due before my payday. Besides that, I was living paycheck to paycheck. My check was spoken for long before it even came. So, I did what I always did whenever I was in a crunch, I called Momma. She gave me the money, but not before giving me a sharp lashing with her words…"Why do you associate with those kind of people?! That girl doesn't care anything about you. She just used you. I just don't understand that." It was one of those times when Momma could say, "I told you so." She was right all along. Her maternal instincts were working when she first met Grace in Tassafaronga. As far as she was concerned, Grace was bad news from the gate.

It was also one of those rare instances when Momma, my biggest fan, was extremely disappointed in me. I spent my whole life wanting her to be proud of me, especially after I became pregnant at sixteen. I also felt that making her proud was the best way I could ever make up for her diabetic condition that I believed was caused by the news of my pregnancy.

I was able to keep most of the other things I did that would have equally disappointed her, well hidden. But in this case, if I didn't come up with the money quickly, I stood a good chance of going to jail. I couldn't take that chance. I had to go to the only person who I knew would help me. Everything she said about Grace was right. Grace wasn't willing to pay any part of the money back, insisting, whenever I brought it up, "I don't have any money."

Several years went by before Grace resurfaced. By this time her son was in prison, and now she wanted me to write a character letter. Against my better judgment, I wrote it. I hadn't yet grown to the point where I stood my ground. As the saying goes, "If you don't stand for something, you'll fall for anything." I fell for her pitiful plea, and I had to really stretch to find something decent to say about him. Later, she and I had strong words because I was growing in a totally different direction, and the jealousy from her was apparent in our conversations. We had words…I screamed… she hollered…one of us slammed the phone down first, and that's the last time I ever heard from her. The last I heard, she had moved into a nice home with a government voucher, and she was still on a mission to get her first born son freed from a life sentence.

Soon after the whole postal incident, I enrolled in a new type of training program—bank teller training, which would have been pointless had I been given a record. I completed it a few months later with flying colors, and got my bank teller certificate. My first interview after I completed the school was at Crocker National Bank in San Francisco. I aced the interview and was hired on the spot. I loved being a teller, and I was excellent at it. Not long after I started working, my manager gave me a mobile teller drawer so that I could move around and service every window, from the regular window, to the merchant window, to the foreign exchange window, to the gold card window. My favorite days to work were on customer paydays, usually the 15th and the last day of each month. The line would wrap around the rotunda of the bank. Several customers would wait for me because I was friendly, fast, and efficient. I got a thrill from saying, "May I help the next customer in line."

While my coworkers grumbled about the line, handling so much cash, and never balancing at the end of the day, I was loving it… swiftly and eagerly counting out my cash drawer each day, and balancing to the penny every time. I've since concluded that the reason I loved that job so much was because I was passionate about interacting with people from all walks of life, and giving something to them that they considered valuable—in this case it was the deposit or withdrawal of money. Later, as my self-awareness developed, and as I advanced in my education, my career would evolve into helping clients with deposits into the quality of their life.

I continued receiving Daddy's Social Security for a short stint while I was not in school. Social Security got wind of it, and they started garnishing his monthly benefit. Though we very rarely talked after he left Oakland when I was 11-years-old, he never failed to call me and remind me that I needed to pay the money back. He would constantly say, "I'm on a fixed income, I don't have the money to give back to them." I thought maybe he would pay it to compensate for all of the money he didn't give to Momma to help her care for us, but he never did. Finally, I paid the money back to Social

Security, and Daddy was satisfied. He even sent me a Mother's Day card after that. The one and only card I ever received from Daddy.

Eventually I returned to college to pursue my bachelor's degree. A typical day in school kept me busy and out of trouble. By the time I got home, all I had time to do was take care of Little Mario, cook sometimes, pay bills, then do homework at night and get ready for the next day.

Once in a while on the weekends, my friend Vickie and I would go out. Her mom happily kept Mario for me, and with her I knew he was in good hands. Just like back in high school, Vickie knew where all the good parties were. So we piled up the girls in the front and in the back…at least six deep, and off to the party we went. This was before seat belt laws and common sense kicked in. The house parties were usually in the affluent neighborhoods, primarily in the hills of Oakland, Berkeley, Kensington, or El Cerrito.

At 19-years-old, though I was book smart, my common sense still hadn't quite kicked in. At least not enough to warn me that just because an animal was adorable, it didn't mean that I should have it, or more importantly, that I could afford to properly take care of it. My son's father's best friend, Irvin, and I, bought two darling little Alaskan Eskimo puppies. We named them Precious and Pleasure. He took Precious and I kept Pleasure. I can't remember where and why we bought them, but I remember they were irresistible…Lord knows I didn't need a dog.

My son's father found an additional use for Pleasure. She was a "chick magnet." So, he and Irvin would often take the dogs for walks. While Mario was tall, dark, and handsome, and the puppy I guess enhanced that, Irvin was "eye candy" with or without the puppy. He was single, so the fact that he and my boyfriend were so close caused a lot of problems. One day Irvin met the young woman he'd spend the rest of his life with, Vita. At that point he completely turned his life around, which included distancing himself from Mario. I thought that might be a wake-up call for my son's father, but instead, he continued with his dirty little schemes.

Mario would continue to walk Pleasure and meet girls. Especially around Lake Merritt in Oakland, where hundreds of teens would gather on nice days. It didn't matter that this was a place I would frequent too. Other than the fact that he was lurking around somewhere, it was a good time. My friends and I would go to the lake and sit on the grass all day. We'd people watch, talk, mingle, play music, and watch others show off their fancy cars as they drove slowly in a line of cars around the lake. We would always have a good time…without any trouble. For at least a couple of years on nice days that's where I'd be with friends on the weekend. That is until the neighbors decided we were a public nuisance and the police put a stop to it.

By this time, I had a car. It was a forest green 1970s Ford Pinto. I paid all of $300.00 for it. Right after I purchased it, a report came out that the gas tanks were defective and if in a rear end accident, the car could blow up upon impact. You would think that would have been enough of a warning for me to use it with caution, or perhaps not at all.

Vickie and I graduated from teenage house parties to night clubs and "over twenty-one" parties. We went everywhere from Silks in Emeryville, to Dock of the Bay in Berkeley, to Wine and Roses in Jack London Square, and even as far as to Studio West in San Francisco. Most of us, if not all of us, were under age. We had a strategy to get past the guy at the door that worked every time. One of us flaunted a little skin, another smiled kindly, and one of us talked very sweetly about how badly we wanted to get in the club. Not only did we get in, but whenever there was a cover charge, we rarely had to pay it. It didn't hurt that we were all nice looking girls, with curves in all the right places. By the time we were old enough to get in the twenty-one and up parties, the party promoters got smarter. They started putting females on the door. But that wasn't our problem anymore.

My son's father went to Los Angeles during this time, for God knows what. He called and asked me if I'd come out there, and if I did, to bring his television when I came, which I'm sure is all he really wanted. The thought of going to Los Angeles for the weekend sounded like fun, and a welcome change. I called Vickie, who was my "down for everything" friend, and we packed our bags. We gathered up Little Mario, who was 2-years-old at the time, and my little dog Pleasure, and we headed to Southern California—a five hundred mile trip. What were we thinking? We weren't. Neither of us had ever driven more than about fifty miles one way, at any one time.

My first mistake was thinking I could drive all the way in the fast lane of the highway doing the 55 mile per hour speed limit. Cars and trucks were repeatedly tailgating me, blowing their horns, getting over, and passing me up. But I couldn't imagine why. I was doing the speed limit. Eventually a red pickup truck was coming so fast that he couldn't stop. We'd only been on the road for a little over an hour, and the next thing I knew the truck hit us hard from behind. We started spinning out of control until we ended up on the other side of the freeway where cars were coming in the opposite direction. By the grace of God, my car didn't blow up; and in His abundant blessings, there was a break in the traffic that allowed us enough time to get Mario and Pleasure and get out of, and away from, the car.

After the accident was cleared up, the tow truck driver dropped us off at the nearest hotel, in the town of Gilroy. They weren't willing to let us stay with the dog. We were young, with a toddler, and we promised to be gone in the morning, but they didn't care. It was now dark. We walked until we found a hotel that would take us. The next day we took a Greyhound bus back to Oakland. It was a pretty traumatic experience that we survived by the skin of our teeth.

Vickie was so shaken up by the whole ordeal that she would never talk about it, and she became annoyed if I brought it up. A long time passed before we went somewhere in a car together. When we did, it was to go to the annual Black ski trip which occurred every Martin Luther King, Jr. holiday weekend in Tahoe. By this time Vickie had a car. She was too nervous to drive that distance, so we agreed that I would drive. When we arrived in Tahoe there was light snow on the ground. Vickie had a fit every time I drove over ten miles per hour. She'd holler at me, and a couple of times, she even socked me in my shoulder. Only Vickie could get away with that. Once we arrived at the first party of the weekend, as always, we had a good time.

With the insurance money I received from the accident, I bought a newer model 1980s powder blue Ford Pinto. Of course it was used, and I paid a whopping $500.00 for this one. At least this time it was after the fuel tanks were remanufactured.

When Mario returned from Los Angeles he'd started experimenting with even more drugs, selling larger amounts, and seriously pursuing his pimp career. He was spending even less time with me and his son. After being in this highly dysfunctional relationship since the age of fifteen, I found myself finally getting fed up with him. He continued smoking Angel Dust daily. His behavior and his personality were changing dramatically for the worse. I was finally figuring out that I couldn't change him, and I was tired of trying.

He kept going back and forth to Reno to buy and/or sell drugs. One day, when Little Mario was almost 3-years-old, he told me he was moving to Reno for good. For the first time, realizing this relationship was a lost cause, I wished he would go.

By the time the weekend rolled around, after working and studying all week, I welcomed Vickie's invitation to go out with some friends.

Her car was on the blink, and on this one particular evening it was freezing cold outside. The heater in my car was not working, nor was the defroster, but it took a lot more than that to stop us. We piled into the car and went over the Bay Bridge to a nightclub in San Francisco that everybody was raving about. If it was cold in Oakland, it was twice as cold in San Francisco, but that didn't matter. Once we arrived, we talked our way in. There was a nice crowd, the D.J. was playing everything we wanted to hear, and the atmosphere was good. We had a great time, and we danced for hours.

The club lived up to all the hype. Around 1:00 a.m. we were tired and ready to go home. As we were preparing to leave, a very nice looking, well-dressed young man came up and introduced himself to me. He said his name was Reggie, and asked what my name was. After I told him, he asked me to dance, and I explained our leaving situation. He then pleaded with me to dance. He was quite charming, and his good looks attributed to my decision to give in. By the time we were on our way to the dance floor, the song switched from a fast song to a slow song.

After we danced, we held idle chatter. He walked with me out to the parking lot. My girlfriends were ahead of me, trying to stay composed while enduring the cold weather. I allowed him to kiss me on the way to the car. My friends were losing patience with me. They were ready to go. We exchanged numbers, and the girls and I proceeded to the car and drove back across the bridge in the chilled San Francisco air, with all the windows down as a makeshift defroster. Distracted by what just happened in the parking lot, I didn't notice the cold as much as they did.

When we first started dating Reggie would pick me up in his shiny new Buick Regal. He cherished that car. After meeting me, the Buick took second place in his heart…but it wouldn't be long after Reggie won me over, that the Buick would be back in first place.

After our first date, Reggie walked me to my door. As we got off of the elevator right across from my unit, I was shocked to see Little Mario's father waiting for me to come home. I thought he'd moved away to Reno like he said he was doing a week earlier; but there he was sitting on the floor in front of my door. He was shocked too, because from the time we started going together when I was fifteen, until the week before that night, he'd never seen me with another man. In that four year period, even with the abuse I suffered at his hands, I never considered being with anyone else. I could tell right away that he was high, surprised, and jealous.

Not wanting any trouble, I told Reggie to leave, and assured him I'd be okay. Reluctantly he left, but I noticed out the window he stayed around, sitting in his car for a little while before actually taking off. He wanted to protect me, but I felt the need to protect him. My son's father was quite a bit taller and he was high. There was no telling what he might do.

He came in and sat on the couch. I sat down on the couch, as far away from him as I could get. I thought we were going to discuss what he just saw. I was ready to tell him it was over. Unbelievably he started to cry. Before I could get comfortably seated on the couch, he balled his fist and he hit me hard in the head. Without a word he got up and left. I called the police, and when they finally arrived, one of them said in a very nonchalant manner, "She's just going to take him back in a few days," as if I weren't in the room. The other officer agreed, and then they left without taking a report, without any protection, without respect, without anything; and their assessment of the situation was incorrect. I never went back to him. In fact, almost exactly one week prior, I had met the man that I would marry and have a daughter with…not necessarily in that order. Nonetheless, Reggie and I would spend the next eleven years together.

A few days after Mario hit me in the head and walked out of my apartment, he came back. Outside of the door to my apartment, he begged me to see his son, and said he was leaving for Reno for good this time. Our son was asleep in the room. Against my better judgment, I let his father in. Because we had nearly a four year history of breaking up and making up nearly once a week, he thought that's all this was. Instead of hitting me, this time he attempted to touch me. I pushed his hand away. He tried to kiss me. I backed away. That was new to him. I was hoping he'd take the hint and go. He was making me sick.

Instead of leaving, he began strong arming me. He pushed me into the bedroom and down on my bed, across from where our son was asleep on his twin bed. I tried with everything I had to get him off of me without waking Little Mario up, but he was too strong. He had all of his body weight on me, and he held my small wrists together with his long fingers, while he forced my pants off with his other hand. He then forced himself on me. I just surrendered and laid there lifelessly until he was done.

After he was satisfied, he got up, fixed his clothes and left. I was humiliated. I felt dirty and used. I sat up on the bed and cried and cried. It's strange, but I don't remember Little Mario waking up through all of that. I don't think he did, unless that's another painful incident blocked from my memory. He was barely 3-years-old. If that wasn't horrible enough, his father had an STD, which was the only thing he left me with. For a long time, I never considered that he raped me. Instead, I just chalked it up again to what was normal…for me.

Fourteen years went by before my son would see his father again, when he was 17-years-old. I'd heard through mutual friends that Mario began shooting drugs intravenously and pimping girls on the street.

Seven years had gone by since the incident in Los Angeles when I became intoxicated at 12-years-old. A lot happened in those years. As I sat on my couch reflecting one evening, I thought about the order in which some of the most significant things happened—I had a baby; my mother left me and James while I was still in high school; I moved on my own and raised my son alone in a crime ridden, drug infested housing project; I graduated from high school; I started experimenting with drugs; I took my first drink since the incident in Los Angeles; I moved again; I broke up with my son's father; he nearly knocked me out; he raped me; and I was now a single mother in college, while working in order to make ends meet.

On the weekends, having two or three cocktails, or glasses of wine took the edge off the sadness I felt. When I would go out with friends, it gave me that confidence that I lacked. It even took away the stress from all of my responsibilities. Like my mother, I held my alcohol well. As obstacles continued to mount in my life, I would drink and experiment with other mind-altering substances trying to take the edge off…escape from my reality…and ease all the pain.

.

Success Principle Ten—Developing Courage

It takes courage to step out on faith, and then wait, and respond with tact, logic and sensibility to any outcome. The courage to be quiet is an acquired skill. It requires courage to listen, especially when tensions are high. The more heated the dialogue, the more empathy and patience that is required in the process.

Having courage means doing something in spite of any fear you may have. Fearfulness is a learned behavior, based in our mind, and reinforced by the outside world. When we have difficulties in life, courage can be much more difficult to display than weakness. But remember that it is only in times of difficulty that our courage is developed.

If you live for any significant amount of time, you will face troubles that only courage will get you through. Having courage is what it takes to deal with challenges—face them, confront them, and learn to grow from them.

There are always valuable takeaways in every difficulty that you make it through. You just have to be open to discovering what that is. If you run, or sweep the problem under the rug, you will never get the lesson that it came to teach you.

Success Tips

❖ Developing true courage requires interaction with difficulties

❖ Don't get stuck in or fight your fear, face it, so that the fear begins to dissipate.

❖ Having the courage to work through fear and get beyond it, is about retraining your mind.

"The happiest people are those who do the most to make others...happy"

—Booker T. Washington

What I've Learned from my Great-Grandfather's life

I would rather be happy than upset on any given day. So, I deliberately set out to do what I can to make someone else's day brighter, even on days when I may not be having the best day myself. It often only takes something as simple as a smile, a compliment, a kiss, or a hug.

Eleven

Irreconcilable Differences

Reggie was at my place all the time, and we went out on dates often. In the infatuated, beginning stages of our relationship the only time he wasn't at my place was when he was at work, or when he was out playing pickup basketball, and occasionally when he went out with his friends. All other times, my happiness was his primary concern...and I was comfortable with that.

The first time he spent the night with me, his mother was so worried because he didn't tell her he wasn't coming home. He'd never stayed away all night before without letting her know. In the morning she called the police to report him missing. When the police asked for his age, she said, "Twenty-one." Puzzled, they told her there was nothing they could do. He hadn't even been gone for twenty-four hours yet.

Compared to my son's father, Reggie was quite an improvement. He made an honest living working hard at General Motors. He never touched any substance other than alcohol, although at times that was a bit too much. He had no aspirations to chase women, and he was fun-loving. He loved to go out on the weekend. When he wasn't with me, I never suspected he was out to find other women, but rather, to have a good time with his friends…and more than that, to be seen. He knew he was nice looking, and he wanted everyone else to know it too. From the time Reggie and I became a couple, everyone deemed us perfect for each other.

He and his older brother were star athletes in high school. He was a sports fanatic and sometimes I felt he obsessed about his past. With his and his brother's talent, I never understood why they did not pursue athletics beyond high school. Possibly, like me, the external support was lacking.

When Little Mario was about to enter the first grade, my name came up on a waiting list for a rehabilitated Victorian under a low income housing program. This was the first time I lived in a 2-bedoom since I'd been on my own. It was still government assistance, and it wasn't in the best West Oakland neighborhood, but it was far from the worst. I was ecstatic about the brand new paint, cabinets, carpet, the long hallway, and high ceilings.

By this time, my Pinto was on its last leg. I would park it in the driveway at night, and mysteriously in the morning it would be on the other side of the street, having rolled out of the driveway as if it grew new legs. That was just one of my Pinto's many problems. I never forget where I came from, and as such, I was never too proud to catch the bus, and even if I was, I had no other choice.

Thanks to Momma, Little Mario was enrolled in St. Patrick's school in West Oakland. Momma always thought private school provided a better education. She was too tired to pursue that for me when I was growing up, but with my son she seemed to have gotten a second wind. As long as I took care of all of the paperwork and other school business, including teacher meetings and after school care, she gladly paid the bulk of his tuition.

Fortunately, Little Mario was very smart and independent in the first grade. He and I would catch the bus in the morning to the West Oakland Bart Station where I'd get off to go to work in San Francisco. He would stay on and go a few more stops by himself, ring the bell, get off the bus, and walk a couple blocks to his school. At that time it was safe to do that, but not now.

One day Momma and I went to the Chevrolet dealer downtown Oakland where I picked out a "brand new to me" used Chevy Nova right off the lot. It was a beautiful emerald green with dark green interior. It was immaculate inside and out, with a new car smell. Momma cosigned. It was my first car note and I never let Momma down. I paid every note on time, until it was paid off two years later.

My mother was definitely a life saver on many occasions at that time in my life. Soon after I got the car, I turned 21-years-old, which was no big deal for me because I'd already done just about everything you can do at that age.

Soon after I moved into the Victorian, Reggie moved out of his mother and step-father's house for the first time, and he moved in with me and Little Mario. At General Motors, he was making good money. I was working at the bank, and though I was no longer receiving welfare and food stamps, I still qualified for subsidized housing. I knew I needed to report the additional income I received from Reggie living with me. But I didn't because I feared there would be a significant increase in the rent, or worse, I would no longer qualify to live there. I was finally beginning to live a more comfortable life. Or was I?

The guilt of lying and cheating the system haunted me until the day I finally came clean, more than a year later. *Why is it that we often think it's easier to get away with doing wrong, when in the long run, it always catches up to us? And most of the time the consequences of our choices are a lot heavier than the ease we experienced from doing wrong.*

Not long after Reggie moved in with me I became pregnant. I was hoping this time to have a girl. Throughout my pregnancy my doctor kept referring to the baby inside my stomach as, "he" even though he knew how desperately I wanted a girl. So I was somewhat disappointed. I was a girly-girl, and I thought that was enough to make me a good mother to my next child. I still had no idea what it took to properly raise children.

Because I didn't dilate far enough when I was pregnant with my son, and I had a Caesarean, the doctor explained that it was highly likely that I would have to have a Caesarean again. So he gave me a choice to see if I could have the baby naturally, or if I wanted to pick a date to have her by Caesarean. I was both afraid and relieved. After surviving the first surgery, I couldn't conceptualize a baby, who was a lot larger than its exit, coming out of me the normal way. I chose to pick the birthday. I picked June 9th, because it fell between the birthdates of my father, and Reggie's late father, my unborn child's two grandfathers.

This time my child's father was in the room with me. In fact, when he got too close so he could see what was going on, someone on the medical team asked him to step behind the curtain that was placed there to block him from seeing the full surgical procedure. The operation involved removing my uterus and placing it on my stomach.

When the doctor took my baby out of my womb, they told me she was a girl, I squeezed her father's hand as hard as I could. It was one of the happiest moments of my life! I named her Regarah, pronounced, Ruh-jair-ruh. It is a combination of both her parent's names, Reggie and Sarah. I chose the middle name based on how I felt about my new little daughter—Angel. Swearing she'd never be in pants, I bought her lots of dainty dresses and matching hair accessories. Momma, would often say in her most facetious tone, "Sarah, she's not a doll." No, she wasn't a doll, but she was my princess…*my angel princess.*

When our daughter was five months old, Reggie and I tied the knot in Tahoe. I also reported his income at that time, and as suspected, the rent skyrocketed to the market rate. Although we would have to spend more money, there was something satisfying in being honest, and in making too much money to qualify for public assistance.

Having moved in with me straight from his mother's home, Reggie obviously wasn't sure if he was done sowing his wild oats. He was so nervous before the ceremony that he vomited outside, all over the fresh white snow. Reggie was twenty-four, and I was twenty-two. I don't think either of us was ready for what we were getting into. We didn't realize at those young ages, that our brains still had a little more developing to do before they were fully mature. We weren't as grown up as we thought we were.

As a married couple, we entertained often. We waited until Regarah was 2-years-old to give her, her first birthday party. We invited about fifty people, and nearly all of them showed up, mostly adults. Most of the time we didn't need an occasion to have gatherings at our house. We invited friends and family over for a hearty dinner, cards, dominoes, and sometimes Monopoly. The music was going. The drinks were flowing. The games got competitive. The players always talked plenty of trash. We played lots of rise-and-fly bid whist. When someone got a Boston, they slammed the cards down so hard they made nearly the same sound as the dominos that were being slammed on a nearby table. Often the person who was going out with a Boston, first slapped the card on their forehead, letting it stick there for a second before it fell down to the table.

In these settings, although most of my friends loved Reggie, some found him challenging to be around because he debated everything ad nauseam. My friend Cathy said "He'd argue with the Dewey

Decimal System." That described him accurately. No matter what someone's opinion of something was, he opposed it. It was no different with me. From raising children, to education, to religion, to living in a better environment, my husband's ideas were very different from my ideas. Whenever I expressed my desires to build a better life for us and for the kids, he would say that I was thinking like the White man. All of a sudden he began to selectively claim that he was a Muslim. Yet, contrary to their practices, he partied regularly, drank often, and ate pork.

We started having problems behind closed doors; still, we were the envy of all our friends. Although the honeymoon period lasted a lot longer than my first relationship, once it wore off, things got rocky. Reggie had a good heart, but intimacy got increasingly difficult as his egotistical side surfaced…and progressed. Gradually, the concern he had for my happiness, started to wane. He always loved to dress to impress when he went out to the clubs. But when he started accumulating way more jewelry for himself, than he ever bought for me, my resentment toward him grew. As the years went on, as with any couple that doesn't work on their marriage, our unhappiness got worse.

We began to disagree more and more, and eventually we clashed about anything and everything. I started to become especially annoyed with him when he would go to the barbershop or to different parks to play basketball, and he would always leave Little Mario behind. I didn't realize then that Reggie was also pulling pranks on Little Mario in the name of horseplay, but he didn't find them funny. One prank in particular that Little Mario couldn't shake occurred when he was 5-years-old, in the High Rise apartments on the sixth floor. Playing a bit too much, Reggie hung him by his arms over the balcony for about five seconds.

Mario didn't tell me this until he was 19-years-old. He told me that whenever these things would happen, I was away from home. When he was growing up, Momma always made comments on how Little Mario never looked happy. I got offended, irritated, and frustrated by her comments, and I just shrugged them off. Mario never told me when it was occurring. Possibly, like me, he felt it was normal...for him.

Reggie was a child at heart. I used to tease him that I had three kids instead of two. His childlike nature made me give him the benefit of the doubt, instead of believing he was callous to me, and especially to my son.

I attribute my staying so long to a few things—we had a daughter; he told me that he loved me often, and that I was pretty at least once a day, every day; and throughout the day he would kiss me affectionately on my cheek. But if I asked him why he loved me, he'd say, "Because you're so pretty." That was never enough for me. I longed for a deeper reason, but I never got it. I often dreamed of what it would be like to have love first, then marriage, and then children after we planned for them.

Another reason I stayed with Reggie so long is because his family embraced me as their own. They had a big family, and this was my first time experiencing family in this way. Most of the older generation were in long time healthy and happy marriages. Those of that generation who weren't married were widowed. They actually liked each other and wanted to spend lots of time together. Not just the married couples, but the immediate family, and the extended family, as well—including aunts, uncles, in-laws, first, second and third cousins. Once when his grandmother and grandfather, who everyone endearingly called Momma Ola and Daddy Connelly, came to visit from Texas. I was moved to see how Momma Ola would happily go about preparing three hot meals for her husband—breakfast, lunch, and dinner—and not just simple meals; for lunch, she fried chicken for him.

One other behavior I wasn't used to was how my mother-in-law always inquired about her adult children's day, after they got off of work. And she truly appeared interested. Sadly, that was unbelievable to me. I'd never witnessed a family where so many members so richly demonstrated their love toward one another, and toward me. Many of them, especially the older members, migrated to California from the Deep South. They were rooted in Christ, and it showed.

We spent every Sunday at his mother and step-father's home for a big Sunday dinner. We spent all of our Thanksgivings at his uncle and aunt's home in San Francisco. Every Fourth of July we went to a cousin's home. The love in the air was so thick.

As fate would have it, or bad karma for not disclosing my full household income, while we were living in the Victorian, Reggie was laid off from his job. Instead of just me and Mario, now there were four mouths to feed. Reggie began working odd jobs here and there, and each was a huge cut in pay compared to the money he had made at General Motors. The comfortable lifestyle we had soon turned into me carrying him.

After several months of being laid off from General Motors, Reggie was eventually called back. What a blessing…or so I thought. When he went back and started making lots of money again, he decided he wanted to split our bills down the middle so that he could buy more things for himself. That hurt. He made a lot more money than I did, and I carried him while he was laid off. That was the first time I saw that side of him…a selfish side. But it wouldn't be the last.

I loved my job at the bank, but it was time for me to move on and make more money. I wanted to move out of government subsidized housing for good. I started applying for positions at large corporations so that I could not only make better money, but so that I would have good benefits. I put in applications at Chevron, AT&T and Pacific Gas and Electric Company (PG&E). Friends tried to discourage me by saying I had to know someone to get into those kind of corporations.

When people tell me I can't, something inside of me urges me to prove them wrong. I once heard Serena Williams say, "No's propel me to succeed." I could truly relate to that. I was called by AT&T first. I interviewed, and I got the job as an account representative. I was still in the training phase of the job when I got a call from PG&E. I was reluctant to go on the interview because I already had a decent job with AT&T. I decided to go anyway, and after three interviews—the first with human resources, the second with the department's director, and the third with the immediate supervisor, I landed the job. I started working in PG&E's corporate offices in San Francisco's financial district. I was a Statistical Identification Coder, in PG&E's Economics and Development department... making a lot more money than I'd ever anticipated at that time in my life.

After five years I was vested and qualified for a pension. They paid for me to finish my undergraduate education, which helped to move me into a management position as a corporate account representative. My biggest fan, my mother, was again extremely proud of me, saying "She wished she had a pension." I didn't realize what a pension was before she raved about my having one.

When my daughter was 3-years-old, and my son was 9-years-old, Reggie and I bought a house in East Oakland, off of 55th Avenue. The street we lived on was a low to moderate income, quiet working class block. I was 25-years-old and my mother again was so proud of me because, as she put it, "When I was your age, buying a house was the furthest thing from my mind." After the house, we traded in my Nova, and purchased a brand new glossy, crimson red Saab, with all the bells and whistles...straight off of the showroom floor. It was a five-speed with a sun roof and automatic windows and locks, and a Bose stereo.

While the house and the car were great additions to our material items, they were no match for what we lacked in emotional and spiritual maturity; not to mention our completely different views on parenting and future goals.

I did get to see a very caring side of Reggie when it came to Little Mario. One afternoon Reggie, Regarah, and I went to the mall and Little Mario begged me to let him stay home and ride his bike. Reluctantly I gave in. On our way home later in the day, I fell asleep in the front seat of the car. As we turned the corner onto our block, Reggie noticed an ambulance a few blocks down and a crowd was around it. He knew I was nosey, though I could not look at the slightest drop of blood; yet I liked to know what was going on when emergency vehicles were near. But he decided not to wake me.

As we pulled into our driveway, before we could get out of the car, one of my son's friend's ran up to us and started saying frantically, "Mario, Mario…he was hurt up the street…he fell off the back of the ice cream truck!" Scared to death, I asked Reggie to hurry up and go down there to see what happened. He immediately left. I was hyperventilating. I reluctantly started down the street. Once I got there Little Mario was already in the ambulance, and Reggie was in the back sitting next to him, assuring me that everything was okay.

I followed them to Children's Hospital. Fortunately, he didn't suffer any broken bones, and he was released the same day. We just had to watch out for him because he hit his head pretty hard, and they said he shouldn't go to sleep for a while. They instructed us to wake him every few hours once he did go to sleep. I don't know what I would have done had Reggie not been there for him, and to assure me he was going to be fine. Little Mario later told me he was so afraid until Reggie showed up. And when I came, it just reinforced he'd be okay.

It turned out that Little Mario, being his usual adventurous self, had jumped on the back of the truck. Witnesses believed that the annoyed ice cream truck driver purposely stepped on the gas to cause the kids to fall off. We could have sued, but I didn't have the energy, and I was just thankful that my son was okay. Unfortunately, after we got past that incident, Reggie went back to treating Little Mario like a "step-child," which is what he was to him; but even so, it didn't have to be so obvious.

Once again, I found myself in a relationship that was going nowhere. Only this time, it was a more gradual decline.

Reggie and I began going out separately, more and more often. My mother was always baffled at our relationship and how often we'd go out without each other. She was even more troubled by the fact that the invitations we'd receive in the mail were for parties we had to pay to get into. She would say, "In my day, if you were invited somewhere, you certainly weren't expected to pay." That actually made a lot of sense, but nonetheless, it was a new day.

Most often, his mother would keep the kids when we went out. I'm not sure if she wanted to, at least not so often, but she did it anyhow. Her son and I were in our own little worlds and didn't give much thought to what we were doing to her, or the kids. At other times he'd go out on Friday and I'd go out on Saturday, or vice versa. That way we didn't have to find a babysitter, or let his mother know just how often we were going out, instead of being with the children.

My late mother-in-law was one of the kindest, sweetest ladies I've yet to meet. She and her daughter were as different as night and day. The daughter emotionally abused Regarah. Always demeaning her and putting her down. She was also mean to Mario, but he didn't go over there as much as Regarah did, since they were not his blood relatives. Because of the way she treated my children, Regarah's aunt and I had more verbal fights than I can count. One of the worse was when Regarah was around 10-years-old, and I asked her not to use a straightening comb on her hair because she was too young. When I picked her up the next day, her aunt had given her a relaxer. I was livid. I didn't stop going out on the weekend, but I did find alternative care for my daughter.

When Regarah became an adult she told me that her aunt gave her alcohol once when she was just 9-years-old. I should have been more concerned about what was going on around my daughter; but the fact is, I wasn't...I had on blinders. Oblivious to what was happening, I continued to leave her there for at least a few of the most formative years of her childhood, while I went out to the clubs with girlfriends, trying to find some solace to the unhappiness festering in my heart.

While we were still living in the Victorian, Reggie met a friend who was working at one of the odd jobs he had when he was laid off from General Motors. They were starting to develop a close bond. His friend was also married. One night, we all went out together. Reggie's friend and his wife were very nice, easy to like, intelligent, down to earth; and each had a great personality and a sense of humor, that made them fun to be around. They were also a very handsome couple. They met while they were in college, and it was obvious they loved and adored each other. We began going out with them regularly. We'd sit for hours, talking, dancing, eating, and drinking. Often we would visit each other at our homes. Our relationship with them seemed to put some of the spark back into our own marriage.

Except for the fact that they regularly smoked weed and we didn't, we had a lot in common. One thing Reggie did not have in common with the three of us, was that we were willing to explore substances beyond alcohol and weed. On one particular evening, we decided we'd get some cocaine, and go to their house instead of going out. Reggie opted to go out. That night was the first of what would become a weekend ritual for the three of us for at least a couple of years.

In addition to the weed and the cocaine, there was also alcohol. I was soon surprised to learn that the husband also used heroin, intravenously. I was shocked because, unlike my neighbor who died from a heroin overdose in Tassafaronga Village, they were both college-educated, gainfully employed, and very high functioning. In fact, we were all high functioning. I never gave up on my dreams about education either.

Despite all that was going on, and even in my brokenness, I found my way back to school to pursue my bachelor's degree. My children remember me having papers all over the dining room table. I never received a grade below a B. I continued to go to work every day; get my children off to school; and all while keeping my weekend life hidden from my family and my closest friends. I think a lot about that. On the outside I appeared happy—but I was far from happy. Something was missing, and I was chasing it, not knowing what "it" was.

Overshadowing the genuine friendship we initially developed, the substance abuse eventually began to take on a life of its own, and it became the glue that held us together. It was also the determining factor that would separate Reggie from the three of us. Reggie started going out on his own again. He always kept in close contact with our friends because underneath the drugs, they were really good people.

Before we began going out with them, our marriage was on shaky ground. The addition of this new flawed situation was no match for our already weak foundation. After eleven years of being in the relationship, Reggie and I mutually agreed to separate. In sharp contrast to my previous relationship, that was the first time we ever broke up in the eleven years together. It was also the last. I helped him find an apartment, and he left. Our daughter was extremely saddened by his leaving. Mario, on the other hand, was rejoicing silently.

Reggie and I were separated for three years before we divorced. We didn't want his mother and step-father to know because they would be devastated. Somehow when we finally filed for a divorce, the papers fell out on their front lawn. My mother-in-law found them and picked them up. As we suspected, she was extremely hurt. Our friends were also shocked and in dismay.

I continued going to visit the couple my husband introduced me to, and we continued to self-medicate. As with anything that is far from "right living," although we started out with what seemed a genuine friendship, the drugs began to create a dysfunctional relationship between us. When there were drugs, we were good; but the negativity between us became very clear when there were no drugs around. We were all working, and able to make sure that was never for too long. What started out on weekends only, turned into the weekends, plus a couple of days during the week.

Though it may not have taken a toll on our employment or my academic life, eventually, the dysfunction began to take a toll on not only the three of us, but in the lives of our children. Soon I found my checking account depleted, my savings account wiped out, and my credit cards maxed out. Several times I made a desperate attempt to quit, but I would revert back again and again. A few times the husband tried to join my battle for freedom, but his addiction was too far gone to do it on his own.

I once accompanied him to a recovery meeting. It was in a dangerous part of East Oakland, which was ironically across the street from one of the places he bought heroin. We were the only two who appeared groomed and dressed in nice clothes. The people seemed to think that we thought we were better than they were, or maybe that was just my imagination. Some of the regulars seemed to shun us and make snide remarks accusing us of interfering in their real plight to overcome their addictions. Perhaps it was just an unconscious excuse for us to not come back, because the demon won him back and eventually me also.

Nothing could have prepared me for the day I answered the door, and it was my friend. She was beyond distraught. She came in and relayed to me that she came home and found her husband, my friend, dead…from a heart attack, she said. From my phone she called his mother, who he was extremely close to. All I could hear on the other end of the phone was a long, loud, high pitch scream, blaring a resounding, "Nooooo." He was her youngest of two children.

Earlier that day I'd stopped by their house. He was home alone, and when he opened the door I could tell he was getting high. Because we were trying to stop, I left very disappointed. I would have given anything to have been able to relive that moment. But I don't know what I could have done differently. Following his funeral I attempted to use again. Fortunately for me, God intervened. Though I am a strong advocate for programs, more than twenty-years later, without a program I have not used or craved any drugs since then.

Success Principle Eleven—Coming out of the Storms of Life

There is a saying that goes, "Life is what happens when we are busy making other plans." The storms of life are unavoidable. Most likely we are either facing one, just getting past one, or we are on our way to one. Equipped with this information, we must be mentally prepared for the storm before it gets here. The good news is, in the storm there is always an opportunity to grow.

It is not the circumstance of whatever storm we are in that shapes, makes, or breaks us, it is our response…our reaction to the circumstance. We can choose our response to every situation we encounter. The choice makes the difference in the type of person we become, strong or weak, powerful or powerless.

When we are faced with situations which are out of our control we must keep our eyes on the lesson and the message— that's where the gift is found. The lesson teaches us how to handle our circumstance, and how to make it through future adversities. The message is the guide we use to teach others how to get through, or avoid, similar situations.

Success Tips

❖ No matter what the situation, you have a choice in how you respond to it.

❖ When you are in a storm, don't wallow in it, keep going until you make it through.

❖ Only consult with those who have successfully come through a similar circumstance.

"He who lives outside the law is a slave. The free man is the man who lives within the law, whether that law be the physical or the divine."

—Booker T. Washington

What I've Learned from my Great-Grandfather's life

High moral character is of primary importance. It is what I demonstrate when I do the right thing when no one is watching. If I cut corners, without concern for doing what is right, but simply for my own benefit, I am convinced there will be inevitable consequences to face.

Twelve
Train Up A Child

Something my father used to say all of the time when I was young was, "This too shall pass." That has always stuck with me. I'd gone through hell and back in the recent years, but I knew I had to keep on going. Shortly after I became a single mother, again, Little Mario began getting more and more mischievous.

One day when I was doing homework, there was a knock on my door. I looked out the peephole, and I recognized the tall, thin older guy on the other side of the door, as the landlord of the apartment building across the street. Irritated because I was on a roll with a paper that was due the next day, I wondered what in the world he wanted. When I opened the door, he explained to me that Mario spray-painted his driveway. He said he was going to get an estimate, and I would have to pay to have it removed.

Already strapped for cash, I didn't need any unexpected expenses. If he could not prove to me beyond the shadow of a doubt, that

Mario did it, I wasn't paying for anything. Annoyed, I followed him outside so that he could show me what he was talking about. All the while I was wondering why he was so sure it was Mario. Halfway across the street, I had my answer. My son spelled his name in the driveway in big red, capital letters—M A R I O. He didn't even try to lie his way out of this one. All I could think of was, "Of all the things he could've written, he wrote his name." He did the deed, and provided the evidence all at the same time. I needed another bill like I needed a hole in the head. I was furious.

I heard about an organization, the Omega Boys Club, which helped troubled young Black boys get on the right track. That sounded like just what I needed. One evening when Mario was 12-years-old, in a desperate attempt to get help, I took him to one of their first meetings at McClymond's High School in West Oakland. The meeting was extremely encouraging. Regarah was six at the time. She and I were especially moved by one of the organization's leaders who had a gift for preaching. Though we were inspired, Mario sat there looking rather bored the entire time.

When the meeting was over, I was excited to go up and speak to the organizer. I explained what I was going through with my son… getting suspended repeatedly for clowning in class, disobeying my rules, spray painting on our neighbor's property, etcetera. He kindly let me know that their organization targeted boys in much more serious trouble—gang bangers, drug dealers, and those committing violent crimes. I was between a rock and a hard place. He was too mischievous for me to do much with…and yet, he wasn't bad enough for them to do anything with. I understood, but I left feeling disappointed nonetheless.

The Omega Boys Club, was just getting off the ground back then, and today they've successfully changed the lives of hundreds of seriously troubled Black youth, many of them graduating from the most acclaimed Black colleges in the country, including the school my great-grandfather started, Tuskegee University.

I guess in a way, I should have been happy that my son didn't fit the bill for their program. Still, I was at a loss. How in the world was I going to effectively raise this smart, beautiful, mischievous young Black boy without a father, or a positive male role model, in the middle of East Oakland, where his peers were falling victim to the hard life of the streets day by day?

Even with all the partying going on, I was still concerned about where Mario and Regarah would attend school. The district we lived in was out of the question. Although our block was quiet and mostly working class, the surrounding blocks were very different. Everything from drug deals, to robberies, to violence was going on right up the street. Our neighborhood was increasingly becoming worse. More nights than not, gun shots rang out as I tried to fall asleep on the couch in the living room, praying they wouldn't come through the walls of our house.

Once again, Momma chipped in financially to send Mario to Saint Leo's, not far from where she lived. Mario was deemed a class clown beginning in preschool at Little Learners in West Oakland, and he continued to be the class clown well beyond. I used to try to say it was the teachers, but when they were all saying the same thing, I knew the common denominator was my son. When he was in the fifth grade at Saint Leo's, I'm sure they knew he was a class clown at the beginning of the year; yet they waited until May to expel him, not just from school, but from the entire Diocese. This made it close to impossible to get him into another school at the end of the year. On the bright side, my mother had recently secured a new position as the manager of a brand new independent senior living facility across the street from beautiful Lake Merritt. I began using her address so that Regarah could attend Lakeview Elementary School.

Using my mother's address, I was able to enroll him in Lakeview Elementary School, as well. Once he graduated from the sixth grade, I then enrolled him in Westlake Middle School, which was still in my mother's district. I was at the school almost as much as he was. I would have to plead for him to get back into class or into a new school. He started getting blacklisted by the teachers, making it more and more difficult to plead my case. My pleading escalated to the district. From there I was able to enroll him in King Estates in East Oakland. Very shortly after, he was expelled for unruly behavior—clowning. With no other options, I enrolled him in Havenscourt Middle School in our district. They didn't have a choice, they had to take him.

Though Havenscourt was a rough school with a majority of teachers who didn't seem interested in the well-being of the students, I thought things were working out. I hadn't heard any complaints from the school...that is, until I got a call a few weeks later saying that they hadn't seen Mario in several days. His story was that he was afraid to go to school because a gang of boys were bullying him. Even though he kept getting in trouble, I gave him the benefit of the doubt, and I never gave up on him. But the teachers and principals didn't have the same compassion. I only had two children to worry about, they had hundreds.

During all these transfers, I was without a car because the Saab broke down and it was too expensive to fix. I asked Reggie if I could use one of his two cars. He said plain and simply, "No." I wasn't expecting that answer, especially since part of the reason I needed transportation was to give his daughter a better education. Disheartened, I asked why. He responded, "Because you can't drive." That heartless response hurt me really, really bad. He just blew me off. But again, when others tell me no, it just propels me to succeed...to find a way out of no way.

Every morning I would get up and get myself and the kids ready. During this time, hip hop was on the rise. Even with all the jazz

I grew up listening to with Momma, I was stuck on R&B, funk, and hip hop. Hip hop was just a spinoff of those genres. The artists just added rhymes, poetry, and spoken word to sampled beats.

There was one video that came on every morning, on a cable program called "Soul Beat." The name of the song was, "Up Town Kick'n it." In the video young musical artists, including Heavy D., walked around a boardroom table to the soulful beat of the song. Sitting around the table were several older White men who were making the decisions on their music. It was pretty deep. The beat was energizing, and it became a morning ritual for the three of us while getting ready for school and work.

One morning I heard Snoop Dog and Dr. Dre's, "Ain't nuthin' but a G thang" playing in my son's room. I was pulled into the beat of the song. It became our new morning ritual. We ate cereal and got dressed to it. Then the three of us, plus our cat who traditionally followed us, left and walked to the bus stop, often in the cold, and in the pitch black of the morning darkness, to catch the first of two buses to get to their school. Once we arrived at their school, Mario would take Regarah to her classroom, and I'd catch the bus to work at PG&E in San Francisco. Sometimes I'd drop them off at my mother's if I had to be at work early, and Momma would arrange for one of her tenants to drive them to school.

Just like with my mother and my father, I always had to beg Reggie for the child support. Unlike my father, Reggie always gave it to me. But it was always the very last day of the month, and not a day sooner—no matter how desperately I needed it during the month. Reluctantly, after a few years of begging, I filed through the court. He asked me not to follow through, promising to do better. But it was too late. He ended up having to pay nearly two times more than I was accepting from him before the court order.

Mario started hanging around with the wrong crowd. It wasn't hard. They lived all around us, and there was no positive male role model around to instill in him an alternative lifestyle. He ran away a couple of times, went to juvenile hall, and he became really rebellious and hard to raise. He eventually started selling drugs. In the ninth grade, he dropped out of school.

When Mario ran away the first time I went all over our East Oakland neighborhood, frantically looking for my son. I would yell out his name up and down the streets nearby our house. Much later in his life, he told me that while I was calling his name, and asking if anyone saw him, he heard me from the bedroom of one of his friend's homes. I was only sixteen years older than he was. Convincing him that, despite our age difference, I was the head of our household wasn't easy.

After he ran away the second time, I finally gave in to his paternal grandmother's plea to let him stay there to see if things would change. At the time, his uncle—his father's youngest brother—was also living there with her. For several of Mario's younger years, his uncle would come and take him out trick-or-treating on Halloween. His uncle was a positive role model. He was the youngest of four boys, and he stayed out of trouble.

Unfortunately, Mario's behavior only got worse as he continued to act out; so I had him come back home to live with me. Our relationship continued to be tumultuous. Once he came in with his ear pierced. I went ballistic. The next night he came in with a second hole in the same ear. On a much more serious occasion I came home and caught him in the shower with his girlfriend. Again I went berserk. For the next few years, as his behavior declined, I became more and more distraught. When he turned 17, I surrendered to the notion that I could raise my son alone; but I never gave up.

One afternoon when Mario was 19-years-old, and he, my brother, and I were sitting on the couch in my living room watching television, I suddenly got this brilliant idea. I asked Mario and James, "How would you guys like to rent this house from me and have a bachelor pad?" They were thrilled about the idea. That made it possible for me to move to a better neighborhood with better schools for Regarah.

It felt so good to begin the search for a new environment. I looked high and low, but only in places where there were decent schools for my daughter to attend. I finally found the perfect neighborhood about fifteen minutes away, in Alameda on Shoreline Boulevard— right across the street from the beach. We soon moved into a charming two-bedroom apartment. For the first time, we each had our own bedroom. There was just one bathroom, but it had a double sink. We were moving up.

At the time, I was finishing up my bachelor's degree at St. Mary's College. I remember driving up the street on Shoreline and a feeling swept over me. I got a chill and began thanking God for the change in my life. I only went to church occasionally then, and not for any real value, but so that God could bless me without me doing much in return. Years after I had that chill, and I started attending church on a regular basis, I thought to myself, *That feeling that swept over me must have been His Spirit stirring in me,* because after all I'd been through in my life, living across the street from the beach is not where I expected to end up.

My daughter was just about to turn 13-years-old. Her new middle school was right around the corner from our apartment, and we didn't have to use someone else's address anymore—we could use our own. All was going perfect, but I wasn't prepared for how she'd react to the move. Veering from my plan of starting fresh and exposing her to new opportunities, she gravitated toward the kids who were on inter-district transfer, the troubled kids who came from Oakland's worst neighborhoods. Was the cycle of low self-esteem that started with my mother continuing with my daughter? In hindsight, it is all relative.

For her thirteenth birthday I decided to let her have a sleep-over with her new friends. I woke up to go to the bathroom around four o'clock in the morning. I heard them in the living room making crank calls. I was beyond upset. On that Sunday I was planning to make one of my infrequent visits to church. Before I left, I told them, "By the time I get home from church, everyone better be ready to go home." Thinking back on it, I should have made them go to church with me. But like so many other adults who want peace in their lives, I had it backwards.

When my angel princess got a bad report card, which was more times than not, I blew up. I criticized her choice of friends. I was trying so hard to force her to act something out that I had no idea how to teach her. When she graduated from middle school I dressed her in a pretty, beautiful emerald green satin dress, with matching accessories. I was so excited when they announced her name to receive her diploma. She walked across the stage doing a fist pump. Sitting beside my mother, I wanted to die right there in my seat. There would be many more of those times before she reached eighteen, and lots more after that.

After middle school she attended Alameda High School. One Friday I went to pick her up from school early because we were going on a camping trip with friends. She didn't know I was there. Her back was to me. She was criticizing the cheerleaders, using profanity, and sounding more jealous than critical. I was so hurt, and I was disappointed in how she was expressing herself. Her friends were facing me. Though they could see me, she couldn't. They looked terrified for her, but didn't know how to tell her I was right there. Once she saw me, I read her the riot act. I didn't speak to her all the way on the two-hour drive to the campground. I was so mad at her. I made her feel really terrible, verbally attacking her. I had a knack for that whenever she disappointed me…making her feel really ashamed. After all, she was supposed to be my princess.

My relationship with my daughter, from her birth to her mid-twenties, advanced something like this: It went from "my little angel princess," to, "princesses are not supposed to behave that way," to, "who can help me to teach her how to be a princess," to, "this princess thing is just not going to work." I went from doting over her from around birth to 10-years-old, to having her admitted to a psychiatric hospital in her twenties.

Following in the footsteps of my mother, and then me, Regarah didn't realize how physically beautiful she was. Immediately after I delivered her, I noticed her beauty. She didn't have that newborn look. Instead she entered the earth bright-eyed, vibrant, and glowing. I have a lip fetish, and as a baby, she had the most beautiful and plump lips I'd ever seen.

As she grew up, she began to develop striking features. She once told me she wished she could wake up in the morning, and not need anything like makeup to make her look nice. Those words invoked a lecture from me. That was not unusual. I told her, "Makeup simply defines and enhances your already beautiful features. Besides that, though Halle Berry and Beyoncé look decent without makeup, even they wear makeup to look stunning, to open doors, and to catch everyone's attention…and there's nothing wrong with that."

With my mother's help, I sent Regarah to better schools than the schools in our district, I enrolled her in image development and dance classes. During her performances my mother and I were always front and center, cheering her on. When her dad didn't pick her up as he'd promised on the weekends, as she sat on the porch crying, I was always there to pick up the pieces. I paid for her to go on trips with her dance troop to New York and Florida. I took her to concerts, movies, plays, parks, and beaches. We went camping, and on vacations together, including Disneyland, and a Caribbean cruise.

She was six years younger than her brother. She was a girl, and I thought maybe this was my second chance to get things right. After all, we were of the same gender, and I was a girly girl in every sense of the term. So, this I thought was going to be a breeze. She and I were very close, we often laughed together until we cried at dumb jokes that one of us would tell. We cried tears of joy and we cried tears of sorrow. But somehow that wasn't enough.

I loved and cherished my children from the bottom of my heart. I'd invested so much in trying to give them the best that I knew how. But there was so much that I was unknowingly working against. When they were growing up I went out in the evenings almost every weekend, leaving them with my mother-in-law, where her adult daughter planted seeds that they weren't good enough. Without their buy-in, and in spite of any disapproval, both their fathers left and spent little, to no, quality time with them after that. I continued going out on the weekends. While I did enroll them in positive activities and gave them my utmost support, I only enrolled them in what I wanted them to do. When they failed at something I thought they should excel at, instead of consoling them, I yelled at them; all while their little brains were rapidly developing.

In the process of raising Mario and Regarah, I had no idea, that I was clueless about how to raise happy, healthy, and productive children. I was just going through the dysfunctional motions, doing the best that I could with what I knew at the time. There was no model, and there was no guide.

Unfortunately, I didn't know of the depth of wisdom that could be found right in the Bible. I used to wish that I knew someone who would pick them up and take them to church every Sunday. I wasn't raised in the church, so I was unaware at the time that I needed to take them myself. Even so, I wanted them there with or without me, because I somehow knew it was necessary for living a good life. Like an appliance, you learn how to operate them according to the instructions of the manufacturer. It's no different with us human beings. We have to go to the Source to find out how we should operate.

Success Principle Twelve—Raising a Child's Level of Competence

When children are developing their beliefs about who they are, it's important that they get the whole picture. Too many children only hear what adults think of them when they are being disciplined. In harsh tones they are told that they are *bad,* or that they are *just like their father,* or that they *will never amount to anything.* Additionally, when we discipline harshly and yell at our children, we invalidate them.

In my past clinical work with families, I found that often, parents who are under a large amount of personal stress, tend to take it out on their children. This can be especially damaging if they are inflicting physical punishment. Scolding a child by verbally or physically abusing them is more likely to reinforce the negative behavior, than it is to develop positive behavior.

Children tend to rise to what they believe adults think about them. We need to tell them who they are, and where they come from, and explain that this is the reason we have high expectations for them—and then watch them rise to the expectation.

Success Tips

❖ Empower children by building up their confidence, and not tearing down their self-worth.

❖ Respect the intelligence of children by explaining why or why not there are certain rules.

❖ When disciplining children, separate your personal stress from their punishment.

❖ Label the behavior, not the child, when disciplining them.

"I will allow no man to drag me down so low as to make me hate him."

—Booker T. Washington

What I've Learned from my Great-Grandfather's life

If someone treats me with disregard, I cannot spend my time dwelling on their act. I instead understand that most people who treat others wrong, are victims of their own damaged thoughts...people who are hurting, tend to hurt others. My understanding of this, doesn't mean I have to hang around and be hurt by them. If the bad behavior outweighs the good, I choose to take myself out of the relationship.

Thirteen

Looking for Love in All the Wrong Places

Since the age of fifteen I'd been tied down in two different committed relationships. One for four years, and one for eleven years. Now in my early thirties, for the first time since I was 15-years-old, I was single...with two children to raise. The voice of an accomplished young man giving advice to my brother at a social gathering over ten years ago, advising him not to mess around with women who have children, rang loudly in my ear. Since I'd only been in the two relationships over that long stretch of time, it was as if I were still a teenager, unaware of what makes a healthy relationship. On top of that, my early years of witnessing my father's dysfunctional behavior when it came to intimacy with the opposite sex, created an unhealthy perspective in my mind about how to be in a meaningful relationship with a man.

As well, my mother didn't prepare me for the art of healthy dating. She instilled in me from an early age, "Pretty is as pretty does." From my outward physical appearance I looked and acted like a pretty lady that a man would be proud to wine and dine in public... as well as to become intimate with behind closed doors. Due to my upbringing, the latter was more likely to happen. I just didn't believe I had much to offer beyond my sensuality. I was confident in that area, and I believed that was the catalyst that would eventually bring forth a bonding and happy relationship. But nothing could have been further from the truth.

I attracted a lot of guys, from those who were destitute, to those who were well-educated and financially successful. I wasn't a gold digger. Far from it. I didn't have enough self-worth to even entertain that thought. And even if I did, I'd like to believe I would have had the moral integrity to not chase after someone else's money and material.

When Reggie and I separated, my household income dwindled significantly. I was broke, confused, and I wasn't living right. My own personal view of who I was, continued to spiral downward. This state of mind subsequently led to my attempt to fill a void in my life by searching for love in all the wrong places—especially in flawed relationships with emotionally unavailable men.

After the divorce, I started going out even more than I did before. Whenever my girlfriends needed a party buddy, I was the "go-to" girl. Mario was old enough to stay by himself. I only had to find a sitter for Regarah, and after that...I was ready to go.

When I went out, dancing was actually my first priority. I loved watching others dance, and I loved to dance. Not to slow music, but to the latest up tempo funk, R&B, and later, Hip Hop sounds—Cameo, Rick James, Prince, Dr. Dre., Naughty by Nature, and Bell, Biv, Devoe, to name a few. I was the one always at the DJ booth requesting my favorite single, which they almost never had because they were usually brand new releases. In the eighties, a few of my favorites were: "Single Life," by Cameo, "It takes two," by Rob Base and D.J. E-Z Rock, "Oh Sheila," by Ready for the World, and Salt and Pepa's "Push it." In the nineties, it was: House of Pain's, "Jump Around," Digital Underground's, "Freaks of the Industry," "This is how we do it," by Montel Jordan, and the likes. It was the beat of the music, more than the lyrics that moved me.

Dancing for me was the same as reading was for Momma. It was an escape. I used to get lost in the flow of the beat. When it really got good to me, I would close my eyes, and vanish away—into the rhythm. Guys who went out just to dance, would wait for me to finish dancing so that they could dance with me. I believe my energy on the floor gave them steam. When there was a really good song on, I hated when someone would ask me to dance, just so they could try to make a move on me, and then talk to me the whole time. I would act like I couldn't hear them and keep dancing. Those where the times I would dance with my back to them a lot, which sometimes just made matters worse.

My girlfriends and I only went out to social gatherings where upscale people in the Bay Area would fraternize, that hadn't changed since my high school days. That wasn't because we were chasing money. At least for me it wasn't. But rather, because if we so happened to meet the man of our dreams, the odds were better that he would be gainfully employed. Now, it was one thing for me to be in the same room with these individuals, and quite another for me to engage in a conversation with them. As long as I didn't say much, the inadequacy I felt deep inside would not be exposed. I just wanted to hear good music, have a cocktail...or two...or three, laugh and talk with my trusted friends, and dance...and dance... and dance some more. Whenever I met someone who I felt okay about giving them my real phone number, it almost always turned out to be someone who had more problems than I did. Some say that the things we resist the most, are the very things we create. Somehow I managed to automatically gravitate toward the men who were physically attractive on the outside. However, on the inside they were depthless. They were also equally as emotionally unhealthy as I was, if not more so. Unfortunately, I was intimidated by the men who seemed to be secure, and turned off by men who seemed to be of good character.

Once, during intermission at a concert, I went to the bar and ordered a cosmopolitan. While I was standing there waiting for my drink, I was approached by an older distinguished looking gentleman. He appeared to be in his late forties or early fifties. He was very well-dressed. It seemed more like he'd stepped out of a boardroom, than a concert. He was tall, dark, and handsome—very pleasing to the eye…even to my 31-year-old eye. As I stood there in an above the knee, bright floral print, form-fitting spandex dress, he approached me and said, "May I buy you a drink?" Smiling politely, I replied, "No thank you."

From his mannerisms and his outward appearance, I imagined he was well-educated, and that he was a high level executive some- where. Sadly for me, that conjured up my feelings of inadequacy. I knew as long as I didn't say too much, my outward appearance was enough to make it seem like I was confident. I had good pos- ture, and a lady-like stance. Ironically, that was enough to scare off some of the more shallow men, which this particular man did not seem to be. After introducing himself, he began making small talk…asking a couple of questions, including, "How's your evening going?" and "What do you think about the concert so far?" My answers were polite, but short. After I got my drink, I took a long sip, hoping to gain a little courage to continue this conversation with more confidence. He told me that the seat next to him was vacant because someone didn't show up. He offered me the extra ticket. After a few more sips of my drink, I took him up on his offer. He handed me the ticket and left.

I finished my drink, ordered another; and then I went to tell my girlfriend what was going on. I handed my ticket to the usher, and she led me to the very first row, where he was sitting, front and center, waiting for me. He was in the Bay Area on a business trip.

He came to sell his share of a radio station. He lived on the East Coast, and apparently, he was affluent.

On the following Monday when I arrived at work, there were a dozen long stem white roses sitting on my desk. The note on the card read, "I enjoyed you...Ron." I thought, "Enjoyed what? All we did was talk." In my unhealthy mind, I couldn't fathom someone enjoying my company just for the sake of being in my company. This was too much. He wasn't like the superficial men that I was used to. I didn't know how to respond to him. I even wished he'd go away just as politely as he came. When I told Momma about all of this, she couldn't understand why I wouldn't want to get to know him better. Perhaps it was because I feared that around him, I may not live up to her, "Pretty is, as pretty does" standard.

The next time he came to town, he called me and invited me out with him. He said, "You pick the place, anywhere you want to go." The sky was the limit. Whenever there was an opportunity to be confident, a small voice would creep into my head, saying, "Who do you think you are?" At which time, my depleted sense of who I was would emerge. That voice was there when he asked that question that day, and I responded, "I don't care." Northern California is full of alluring destinations. Why couldn't I have suggested Carmel, or Napa, or Sausalito, or even San Francisco, which was nearly in my backyard...for dinner and a movie, or a play, or to a supper club? I enjoyed all of those things. Most of which I was exposed to at one time or another by my mother, my aunts, or in my marriage. But no, I said, "I don't care." We ended up ordering room service in his expensive, deluxe hotel suite. It was a lovely room, but the next day when he dropped me off at home, I felt cheap. I didn't hear much from him after that. My guess is that he was looking for a little more substance, which at the time...I only wished I had some to offer.

With the Oakland A's, the Oakland Raiders, the Golden State Warriors, the San Francisco Giants, and the San Francisco 49ers, in the Bay Area, there's no shortage of nice looking, professional, yet sometimes, shallow men. We often partied in the same circles as the athletes did. We met many of them, not just from the local teams, but from the opposing teams, as well. I went out with a few of them, but staying true to form, I never really had a quality date, or dinner, or even a movie; mostly we'd meet somewhere—either his place or mine, and I spent most of the time prying their hands off of me. When I think about it, I was lucky that I was never forced to do something I didn't want to do with these men who were near strangers—not to mention they had the strong physical build for their professions as athletes.

Once when I was out with one of my girlfriends, she introduced me to her friend, Diane. Shortly after that, Diane and I started hanging out together, shopping, lunch, and of course, parties. We were both single mothers, we each had two children, and we each had two different personas —one we presented when we were out partying, and one we presented in front of our children.

We had a lot of fun together, and we went out often. She was a little older than me, and a lot more confident. Once when we had an argument because she was being a bit too controlling, she apologized, explaining that she grew up with a father who was a high ranking officer in the military. She, in turn, was a military brat, who followed in her father's footsteps. Not in being in the military, but in giving commands. At the same time, she was a very caring friend. I decided that the good in her outweighed the not-so-good, and I decided to keep her as a friend.

Diane was gorgeous, and unlike me, she knew it. Her light brown skin was a little darker than mine, and her hazel eyes were a shade lighter than my eyes. She had thick shoulder-length copper brown hair, and long slender legs. People often thought we were sisters. She loved fashion and was very particular about her clothes. She always appeared flawless. True to her military upbringing, she made sure I was flawless too. She'd swiftly look me up and down, as if she were inspecting me in a lineup. She would make sure my tags were not hanging out of my clothing, smooth out any small wrinkles, and take her fingers and touch up any part of my hair that may have come out of place. Much to my satisfaction, that told me that she wasn't jealous or competitive. It was challenging for me to be around women who were. I knew at least a few who only felt good about who they were, when they made you feel bad about who you were.

Diane's self-confidence got us through many doors...our cultured attitude and our appearance kept us in. I'll never forget one evening when she came to pick me up to go to a party in Jack London Square, a small restaurant town, near the water on the Oakland estuary. She rolled up in a fancy Jaguar that she'd borrowed from a guy friend of hers. I hopped in, and off to the party we went. We were both in our early thirties, but we didn't look a day over twenty-one. When the party was over, a tall handsome guy started talking to me, and I obliged. He was with a not-so-handsome friend. He said they'd been watching me and my girlfriend all night. Very tacky-like, he announced to me that he played for the Warriors. I guess he could tell I wasn't into sports, and had no idea who he or who his friend was. His friend, who shall remain nameless, was a star player for the team. The one who was hitting on me warmed the bench...but he was cute...though tacky.

The tall, not-so-handsome friend wanted me to introduce him to Diane. When I went to tell her, she was in a conversation with someone else. She took one look at him and quickly decided that she was not interested. I told her he was one of the starting players for the Warriors...she was all over it. So, the four of us made small talk in the parking lot for a little while, and before they left, they told us they would leave tickets for us at will-call for their game the next night.

Diane picked me up early the next evening. Clad in our cutest, sexy but classy, dress-down clothes, we headed for the Oakland Coliseum. When we arrived at will-call, Diane, with her usual take-charge attitude, let them know our names, and explained that the two ball players left tickets for us. We were excited to see where we would be sitting. The ticket agent searched, and searched again, and again, but could not find any tickets in our names, or any tickets left by the two players. I was embarrassed…Diane was pissed. She walked away fiercely. I followed. We jumped into the Jaguar…I thought to go home. She stepped on the gas, and the next thing I knew we were at the entrance to the player's parking lot. I could tell because of all of the expensive luxury cars parked there. She boldly announced to the security guard, "I am 'So-and-so's' girlfriend." He looked at the car we were in, looked at us, and decided that was true. He smiled, and politely ushered us into the lot…great security.

I was at a loss for words as she jumped out of the car, and said, "Come on." I followed behind her in total disbelief and curiosity, as she went through the press entrance with the confidence that I could have only had after a couple of drinks. But we were both completely sober. Our next move was even more insane. We walked right onto and across the court where the players were doing their warm up drills. We went to the nearest vacant seats, and we sat down. Luckily those seats remained vacant, as not to cause embarrassment number two for the night. Each of the two ball players, looked at us in total shock. First of all, they knew they hadn't left the tickets for us, and secondly, how the hell did we come in through their entrance? After the shock, the embarrassment, and the fear wore off—it felt pretty good.

On another evening, while out with a different girlfriend, I met a guy named Vernon, who I ended up being in a two-and-a-half-year relationship with—for two-and-half-years too long. This was the first long-term relationship I was in after my divorce. He seemed really nice in the beginning. He met the physical criteria…tall, brown, and…not bad looking. We danced and talked for most of the night. He asked me if I would take him home because his friend, who he came with, was ready to go, and he wanted to stay and get to know me better.

Vernon seemed like a nice enough guy, and he seemed really interested in me. He was very charming; and he had that "bad boy" edge that would eventually live up to the term. I was attracted to him. As if I was on auto pilot, again I was gravitating to his dysfunction and brokenness. After the party was over, we walked to my car. I was a little embarrassed because although this was the first car I'd ever bought brand new, after the separation I couldn't afford to keep up the maintenance. It was now on its last legs. Nothing worked properly...not the automatic locks, or the 16 valves, or the windshield wipers, or the brakes—nothing worked. Like me, it looked good on the outside, but the inside needed lots of attention. He asked me to tell him everything that was wrong with the car, and I told him.

When I dropped him off at his house around two o'clock in the morning, I missed the first of many red flags to come. His live-in girlfriend was looking out of the window. He got out of the car, and we said our goodbyes. The next day he called early in the morning, and asked for my address. He came over. Mario and Regarah were not home. What began as me trying to pry his hands off, evolved into us being unable to resist one another. With my permission, he totally bypassed the first date—red flag number two. He left on a really high note, and returned about two hours later, clad in blue coveralls, and about $300.00 dollars' worth of car supplies, including breaks, light bulbs, motors for the locks and windows, and several cans of oil. He jacked up the car and spent the next several hours in my driveway taking care of my broken- down car. When he was done, it was like I had a brand new car again. I'd never in my life had an experience quite like that, especially from someone I barely knew.

Finally, I thought my ship had sailed in...that my knight had arrived. I was instantly "head over heels." We started seeing each other just about every day. I figured that whoever the girl was, who was looking out of his window the night I met him, must not mean too much—not if he was doing all of this for me. As far as I was concerned, she was a done deal. Little did I know, the next two-and-a-half-years of my life would be spent on an emotional roller coaster, much like the one I had been on with my son's father. Even though I was in my thirties by now, having been tied down ever since I was 15-years-old, I was making mistakes I should have made and learned from long ago. This man was so emotionally abusive; and I wasted more than two years trying to change him back to the guy I met at the party; and who came over the next day and completely overhauled my car.

Initially I was impressed by Vernon's business sense. He was five years my junior, and he was doing pretty well for himself. He would buy homes and refurbish them. When I met him he owned two modest homes that he had bought and fixed up, one to live in, and one as an investment. He also supervised the maintenance staff for a chain of skilled nursing facilities. He was very smart, but he was somewhat crass, just enough so that I was comfortable to be in his company. He would drink a 40 ounce of malt liquor at night and wake up to what was left of it in the morning, explaining that was to cure the hangover—red flag number three. Had he been polished, or showed signs of real integrity, we would not have lasted anywhere near as long as we did. He'd been in the military, but he had no college. Like me, he was from the hood—South Central Los Angeles. Underneath the discipline he picked up in the military, his rough edges often showed.

After meeting me, he was excited by the challenge to conquer and gain my affections. I'm ashamed of the fact that he had just about won that challenge in a day. I even brought him around my children. He liked them, and they liked him too. He was the first guy after the divorce that I allowed to meet them. My guard was completely down, vulnerable as ever; and I was lost in his game that he probably didn't even realize he was playing.

Early in the relationship he asked me how my credit score was, and how many men I'd slept with, as if he was giving me some kind of employment test—red flag number four. I think because my credit wasn't top rated, and I guess his was; and because he wasn't the only person I'd slept with, which should have been obvious by my two children, he'd determined early on I didn't fit the bill. But he decided to take me along for the ride anyhow. Naively, I held on for far too long.

The girl he lived with moved out. She was sick of me being in the picture. He started missing her, so he went back to her…and then he'd come back to me. She and I would go back and forth with him like we were having a tug-of-war. Every inch of me was emotionally leaning on his ability to hold me up. When he tore me down I would self-destruct in a number of ways—crying, drinking, missing work, withdrawing, and not eating.

My first disappointment occurred the first time she left. I felt that I had won, until one morning after spending an emotionally exhilarating evening with him. Early in the morning the phone rang, and he left the room for about ten minutes—red flag number five. When he took me home that day, I knew something was wrong, and I knew it had to do with the phone call. My insecurities kicked in. This was the first of many heartbreaks to come over the duration of our relationship.

His other girlfriend was just as crazy as I was. Our game of tug-of-war went on far too long. He began seeing her again. *She won.* She got fed up with him and had moved out again. *I won.* He soon began seeing her again and moved in with her. *I lost that round.* He started seeing me again on the side and once she found out she put him out. *I won.* She soon got pregnant and moved back in his house. *I lost.* That's when I got really depressed.

Staying true to his dog persona, when he decided he missed me… he would pour on the charm—always when I was beginning to get over him. He couldn't stand to think of me not wanting him anymore. He was just as insecure as I was. He wouldn't let too many days go by without hearing from me. After about the first year of this, I began to imagine how much better my life would be if he weren't in it. It would take quite some time, and additional support, for me to get the strength to be done with him for good.

She was losing ground, but little did I know the worst was yet to come…verbal, mental and emotional abuse…and new women— red flags six, seven, eight, and nine. One morning I drove past his house and I watched him and another girl coming out of his front door. It was much too early in the morning for her to have been just coming over. I immediately knew she'd spent the night. She watched me watching them. It probably turned her on to see that another woman was so desperate for him. Soon he tired of her and was back with me.

I remember one day when I was at work in San Francisco. He'd done something the night before, which I can't recall what it was, but it really hurt me bad. I worked in the heart of the Financial District at the time. When it was time for me to go to lunch, I roamed about the streets aimlessly, surrounded with all of the hustle and bustle of people going to and fro in my midst. I was like a zombie, numb from crying all night.

After work that day, I took my daughter with me to my mother's house. Momma was so upset at how I was acting. She couldn't stand anything that wasn't okay, so I didn't really talk to her about problems, only about what was good. She thrived on what was good about me and my life. But on this day she took one look at me, and said, "Don't you have any backbone?" That didn't help me. It just confirmed that I didn't. She then went on to describe him as "scum of the earth." Her words made me feel like I was at the point of no return.

To cheer me up, Momma decided to take me to the mall, and then out to lunch. She bought me a chic little skirt, and a blouse to match. During lunch we ordered fajitas. My mother had never heard of them and she had no idea what to do with them. As I sat in my misery, I watched her pile every bit of ingredients on her plate, on top of one small tortilla. I began laughing hysterically. That was the first time I'd felt happy in days. I couldn't stop laughing at the site of her plate. Momma was so refined, and here she had this tortilla sitting under a huge pile of lettuce, salsa, sour cream, and meat. I explained to her that she was supposed to use it all sparingly, so that she could make more than that one gigantic one. I laughed some more, and the laugh was infectious as she and my daughter began laughing too. My mother told me playfully that she did not think it was funny that I could finally laugh at her expense.

Eventually, whatever happened to cause my dismay had passed, and he won his way back to me. It was right around Valentine's Day, yet on Valentine's Day he was nowhere to be found. The next day he came over and made this proposition. He asked if he could temporarily stay at my house while he attempted to save enough money to buy another house. Thinking this would give me some sort of leverage over her, I agreed.

My birthday, which is two days after Valentine's Day, was the next day. We got into a huge fight because I wanted to celebrate and go out to dinner. He told me, "You're just looking for a man to wine you and dine you." He called me a gold digger; yet I'd just agreed to let him stay with me rent free. He went on to say, "You know I'm trying to save money and you're making that hard." *How dare me want to go out on my birthday!* After fighting, reluctantly, we went out and fought out loud in the restaurant all throughout dinner. I ended up walking out. The next day he left to go sponge off of someone else. For the hundredth time, I thought, "If I could only break up with him long enough to get over him." Just the thought of getting to that point gave me hope and positive energy. Yet, it was so hard to get there.

The thing I hated most about myself while I was in that relationship was that he controlled my moods. When I got angry I'd often get violent with him. Once, in a heated argument, while we were sitting on his bed I tried to hit him with my purse, but instead it hit the chandelier. The light cover broke and a large piece of glass stuck in his back. A keloid developed on him from the scar, giving him a permanent reminder of me. Even though I never witnessed my parents having a physical fight, there's little wonder why every physical bout I've ever had was with a male. I just took my parent's behavior up a notch. And I had a lot of practice with my brother.

Fortunately, my children never witnessed any of the psychological abuse that went on between Vernon and me. Although they never saw us arguing, they saw the remnants in my mood after it was over.

Once, in an attempt to make me jealous, Vernon told me that he had a female friend who'd been in his life forever. He described her as being very unattractive, so I never saw her as a threat. Plus he'd only see her when no one else would put up with him. He told me how she never got angry with him, and how she would do anything for him, including fixing him nutritious breakfasts, followed up with vitamins. This was also to let me know I wasn't doing enough. I wasn't interested in outdoing her. In a way, she had more sense than I did. She didn't care about what he did, as long as he came back to her so that she could pick up the pieces. At least she wasn't going crazy trying to change him. Although I didn't have a lot of self-esteem, I had enough to not settle for a relationship where I was only good enough to pick up the pieces. And I went through hell trying to prove that.

Toward the end of our relationship, Vernon came to visit and my daughter's babysitter was at my house. She was openly flirting with him. They shook hands during their introduction, and she held on to his hand about three seconds longer than necessary. Then she went on to compliment him on his firm handshake. Later into the evening they ganged up on me, insulting and criticizing me for feeding my daughter cereal every morning, instead of a hot breakfast. If anyone ever wanted to set me off, they could do so in no better way than to gang up on me.

For some reason, when it came to my tolerance and patience under attack, that was the deal breaker—two or more people condemning me simultaneously. Perhaps it was because of the time I was approached in my house by the gang of girls in Tassafaronga Village. Except, in this particular case, I lost it. I cussed them both out, and then put them out. But not before hitting him in the back of his head with the nearest thing I could find—the phone, breaking the skin, and causing his head to bleed a little. From then on out, he dubbed me the "crazy lady" and vowed to never come around me again. I felt horrible. Not so much because of him, or even what I did to him, but more so because of the energy I continued to expend his way.

He consumed me, he controlled my being. Whenever he was nice to me—a visit, a phone call—I was content. But more often than not, he wasn't nice—and more often than not...I was miserable.

Success Principle Thirteen—Overcoming Bitterness

I once heard a preacher say, "Bitterness is like taking poison, and hoping your enemy will die." That statement resonated with me, as I was overwhelmingly bitter from failed relationships.

For so long, women have been letting others determine their self-worth and their state of mind; my mother was no exception. What she failed to realize, as so many women do, was that what my father thought about her, and the way he treated her, had nothing to do with her, and everything to do with him. Because my mother was my model, I would come to join that same class of women, and endure the same kind of emotional weakness.

When a young girl's father is not there to model for her how a good, decent, man should treat her, she is bound to repeat the behaviors of her mother. If the mother's behavior is positive, that's a great thing. Unfortunately, all too often, if the father is dysfunctional, unless the mother who chose him has done her healing work, she is likely to be broken as well.

Success Tips

❖ Forgiving is more beneficial to the one doing the forgiving, than it is to the person receiving forgiveness, because it is freeing.

❖ Letting go of bitterness creates a space for inner peace, therefore, it is easier to let go of bitterness than it is to hang on to it.

❖ Meditation and prayer are powerful strategies in overcoming bitterness, and other negative energy.

"It is not possible to improve the condition in any race until the mind is awakened and improved."

—Booker T. Washington

What I've Learned from my Great-Grandfather's life

A silver lining in a bad situation can be that the situation led to an improved life. To get to the better side of the bad circumstance, I intentionally improve my life by investing time and/or resources in reading positive material, watching or listening to inspiring entertainment, or seeking professional consultation or counseling whenever I feel the need arise.

Fourteen
A Catalyst for Change

On one particular day I was an emotional wreck and I couldn't hide it. My kids were also affected because when Vernon made me unhappy anyone connected to me got a dose of my negative energy.

Meanwhile, deep in my depression while he was staying true to form, I went to visit my cousin Bonnie in Los Angeles. Immersed in my emotions I needed her bluntness. I never knew Bonnie to mince her words. After I spilled my guts out to her, she said, "You're being stupid. He doesn't care about you." Trying to figure out why I would want to be in a situation like this, my cousin went through a list of reasons of why I shouldn't. Finally, after exhausting everything she could think of, a bit flustered, she said, "He's not even cute!"

During my visit with her, she talked about my interest in unscrupulous men, and then we got into my upbringing. We discussed my childhood. For the first time, I got an inkling that it wasn't normal. We talked about how I was potentially looking for my father's love in all of these unhealthy relationships. She said, "You need counseling." She strongly recommended it. She didn't have to twist my arm. I always considered Bonnie to be one of the most enlightened individuals I knew, both intellectually, and in common sense; besides, I was ready to try anything at that point.

I've never shied away from constructive criticism. Especially when it comes from someone who, like my cousin, is looking out for my well-being. Even when it comes from someone who doesn't have my best interest at heart, I appreciate it as long as it motivates me to do better. My cousin's straightforwardness, although piercing, was exactly what I needed. Believing that counseling was my last hope, when I returned home, I immediately began searching for the right counselor. In my mind, the only counselor who could help me with the level of dysfunction and self-destruction I was experiencing, had to meet strict criteria—they had to be female, Black, and have a Ph.D.

My search turned up Dr. Daniels, an African-American woman psychologist. She was a psychodynamic counselor. Simply meaning, she focused on my unconscious processes as they manifested in my behavior. She didn't say much at all. She prompted me, and from there, I did most of the talking. Miraculously it worked. Every week for about the first six weeks, with tears streaming down my face, the first thing I'd ask her was, "Why is he doing this to me?" No matter how much I wanted her to tell me why, no matter how many different ways I posed the same question, her answer was always the same.

Never veering from her professional demeanor, she'd look me straight in my eyes and say, "I can't tell you why he's doing that to you because I don't know him." Tilting her head and squinting her eyes slightly, as if she were very curious, she would immediately follow up with, "Why are you allowing him to do this to you?" After hearing that for several weeks, one day it clicked. I finally got it. The light went on, and it hit me...I was allowing him to do this...I had the power, but I gave it to him.

Once I understood who had the power, in regard to my relationship with Vernon, the idea began to transpire into other relationships—in social settings, on the job, and with girlfriends. What if Dr. Daniels would have grown tired of my question? I believe I could have asked it a thousand times, and she would have never wavered from her professional demeanor, and her question back to me, "Why are you allowing him to do this to you?" As I continued in counseling she asked questions that prompted a lot of discussion about my past—my father leaving when I was eleven-years-old; my mother leaving when I was seventeen-years-old; and my son's father leaving when he was just three-years-old. Abandonment was big in my life. It was central to my being—or, not being. Abandonment was the key to understanding my behavior in my relationships.

Although I heard it first from my cousin, I realized for the first time the depth of how my childhood was not normal. It simply wasn't right for my parents to leave me. I had never considered that before. I discovered that I had all these obstacles. That's also when I realized that my son's father actually raped me. Without the counselor hardly saying anything the light came on and it opened up my eyes. It was all beginning to make sense. I kept succeeding as far as school; so there was a reason to be proud. Still, all this time I'd been looking at the world through the lens of a broken, abandoned child.

Initially, it was very painful to become aware of all the trauma I'd experienced, but as with any scar, the wound has to be exposed and cleaned up before it can heal properly.

After I'd used the maximum number of counseling sessions covered by my benefits, I started going to see counseling Interns who charged a minimal amount. The only problem was that after they finished their graduate studies, they moved on, and I had to begin working with someone new. Of course, this was not ideal for me because the foundation of my anguish began with abandonment. Still, just having that awareness and insight was helpful, and I was determined to improve the quality of my life. This was my only option, so I kept going. Too many people give up before their break through and I was not going to be among them.

I remember one of the counseling Interns commenting on how keen my insight was. On at least a few occasions, she mentioned that I would make a great counselor, and she asked me had I ever considered becoming a counselor. I hadn't, but the seed was planted that very moment. What I knew for sure about what makes counseling work, is that you have to take what you learn in the counseling session outside of the four walls of the counseling room. It's no different with the church and the classroom. What you learn in those rooms, must be taken outside in order for it to work, and to be effective.

One of the most healing suggestions I received from a counselor was done through guided imagery. The counselor had me close my eyes, and then she said, *"Imagine your parents being tiny enough to sit on your shoulders. As you place one on one shoulder and the other on your other shoulder, imagine what their life may have been like. Think about them as little children."* As I sat there and thought deeply about that, it helped me to shift my anger away from my parents, and forgive them. It was incredibly freeing. Another insight that really helped me was when a counselor said to me, *"You didn't get this way overnight…It happened over a thirty-plus year period, so don't expect to be healed overnight."*

Desperate to reach a point where I felt a lot better about who I was, I added a support group to my healing process. I can remember going to one and complaining about my last relationship. One of the ladies in the group said, "Why do you keep complaining when you're just going to go back to him?" That was another example of someone doubting and criticizing me, and propelling me to move forward…someone telling me what I couldn't do. It also reminded me of the policemen the night my son's father physically abused me. It actually give me strength to start ignoring Vernon's phone calls.

As I initially gained insights about what was the driving force behind my unhealthy relationships I got worse before I got better. I got angry with my parents for leaving me. Before counseling, I didn't realize I had experienced abandonment. I thought I deserved to be left, so that my parents could have a better way of life—away from me. I learned that that was a normal part of the healing process. As I continued in therapy, I learned to accept and know that they were doing the best they could with what they had to give at that time in their lives. I took it out on my mother because she was there.

Toward the end of my young adult years, through counseling, I eventually learned to love myself. I started distancing myself from all unhealthy relationships, not just with men, but with women too. As I continued to grow, I began to develop a low tolerance for women who allowed men to treat them badly, and for female friends who didn't treat me well. On more than one occasion, I was a little abrupt with them, and lost some friends in the process. For some, especially if I believed the relationship was worth salvaging, I wrote letters of apology, or I apologized over the phone. Some accepted and other's didn't. I have rekindled the friendships with all those who are on a growth journey similar to mine. As I continued to grow, I began standing up for myself more tactfully, instead of flying off the handle.

I dabbled in a few short-term relationships with men after the one with Vernon. Most were with men who were emotionally unavailable; but the difference was, I didn't take it personally, and I didn't hang around long enough to see if they would change… five months tops.

As I continue to grow, I now consider myself a "lifetime work in progress."

The drippings of a high quality life that I experienced when spending time with my cousins in the summers, and at my "surrogate" Grandma and Grandpa's home while Momma worked, along with my mother's inability to totally escape her rich heritage, left me with an inkling that maybe I *was* better than I was acting. Without counseling, I don't know if I would have ever realized this.

During my emotional healing process, a counselor once suggested that I begin imagining what kind of man I would want to be in a relationship with. That was similar to the "miracle question" mental health professionals ask today. One version of the miracle question goes like this, "Imagine while you were sleeping, a miracle happened, and the next morning when you woke up all of your problems were gone…what would your life look like?" Along those lines, I did begin imagining being in a healthy relationship.

After my divorce was final, one day when I was driving up the street with my daughter when we still lived in my home in East Oakland, I remember sharing with her a wish of mine. I said, "I wish I could find someone who would love me and accept my children. Someone who likes to travel and do things with me; and it would be nice if they had a daughter too." I still longed to be in a relationship with someone who wanted to be with me just because of me, and not because we had children.

One Saturday, after attending my friend Sherlyn's wedding, I reluctantly went out with a girlfriend. I'd stopped being the "go-to" girl when it came to partying. I was tired of the same old thing, realizing there was not much out there for me. At any rate, I agreed to go to a birthday party that evening in San Francisco. I'd finally gotten to a place where I was no longer trying to repair my broken relationship with my father through unavailable men. I was okay by myself.

When we got to the party, my ex-husband, Reggie, was there. That wasn't a surprise, we often traveled in the same circles. He's still the only one of my exes who I feel comfortable talking to, and having a friendship with. Although I often saw him when I was out, we never danced. This time we did, however. It was even a slow dance to Roy Ayers' "You Send Me," which was a song we had dubbed "our song" during our eleven-year relationship. The dance was all very friendly with no ideas of being more than a dance. We were laughing about something; and my laugh, which others often describe as infectious, caught the attention of a tall, dark, and very handsome man with a nice build and very nice thick full lips.

After the dance with Reggie, I was heading to the bathroom when this guy abruptly stopped me. It was as if he'd lost something, and suddenly found it. That evening I looked rather chic, wearing a long red dress with a deep slit up the front. He said, "I heard you laughing on the dance floor, and I was curious about where that laugh was coming from." Once he found the laugh, he decided he liked what came with it. We started to talk.

One of the first things he told me was that he had a two-year-old daughter, who was currently living with his parents in North Carolina. I wondered why he felt a need to tell me that during a first conversation. He wanted to know more about me, so we talked for a while longer and then we exchanged numbers. He said he'd call me the next day, and we parted ways. He called me a week later. I knew there was growth within me because that didn't bother me; and in fact, I really didn't expect to hear from him at all after a couple of days passed by. But he did call, and we arranged to meet in Jack London Square for our first date.

I had just left the counselor's office, and I was on my way to meet Tony when I received a call from a friend who I met in college while we were both pursuing our bachelor's degrees. We'd gotten really close over the past several months. After earning our degrees, we planned to celebrate by taking a cruise. Our departure date was right around the corner.

I didn't have good phone reception, and I remember being in a phone booth when I called her back. She began telling me that she was not happy with the ship we were going to sail on, or the destinations we selected months in advance. She told me that she wanted to change our destination to somewhere in Mexico so we could sail on a newer ship. My immediate thoughts were that, *I'd never gone on any ship before, so this one would be as nice as any other. And besides we were going to Barbados, St. Thomas, St. Lucia, and Martinique—places where our people lived.* My excitement about the trip was slowly turning into disappointment and anger, as she and I went back and forth over the phone about what our final plans would be.

She let me know if the plans weren't changed she wouldn't be going. This ultimately meant, I either had to find another roommate, or pay for the whole cabin because it was too late to get a refund. At that point in both of our lives, we were not the happiest women in town. We were both struggling with being single mothers and sorting through the rejection we'd experienced from the men in our not too distant past. As soon as we were finished with our conversation, I got into my car and drove away to go meet Tony. I couldn't shake the tears, so on our first date I was an emotional wreck. He was comforting and consoling as he tried to help me figure out what to do in the midst of my anger toward my girlfriend and hers toward me, with just eight weeks left before we were scheduled to go on a cruise we'd already paid for.

Once I got home from my disastrous first date with Tony, I called my girlfriend to see if there was a chance to resolve this fairly. One thing led to another, and before we knew it, we proceeded to call one another out of our names, seeing who could stoop the lowest. We brought each other down by dragging up all of each other's dirt, and bringing up the worst of what we'd confided in each other about. I don't know who slammed the phone down first, but that would be our last time talking for at least a couple of years.

My mother, out of her generosity, agreed to pay for my daughter to accompany me on the trip. At the time, I was planning a big surprise party for my mother's seventy-fifth birthday. I was so thankful for what she was doing for me, that it was very hard for me to contain the secret. I desperately wanted her to know that I was doing something special for her too.

In spite of the drama I was presently faced with, I continued planning this surprise for my mother. At the time, my friend Carmen was an event coordinator for the Asia Foundation in San Francisco. She arranged for us to get a reserved room for the party on the top floor, fifty-two stories high, of the Bank of America building in the Carnelian Ballroom. It was the second tallest skyscraper in San Francisco. From the ballroom, there were magnificent views of all of San Francisco, including both of the famous bridges—the Bay Bridge and the Golden Gate Bridge.

One of my mother's sorority sisters, Mrs. Johnson, contributed the centerpieces for all the tables. They were beautiful vases filled with her favorite flowers—yellow and white daisies. On every table there was a bottle of red wine, and a bottle of white wine. We pulled out all the stops. The waiters waited on us hand and foot. One of her friends commented that this was one of the classiest events she and her husband had ever attended, and considering they were very wealthy, that said a lot.

At the beginning of the evening, we just surprised Momma with her local friends and family, some she hadn't seen for years. They all shouted, "Surprise" as my mother entered the ballroom. Momma was thrilled to death. Once she regained composure, and was seated, the out-of-town guests, including two of her closest friends, Thelma from Ohio and Callie from the Bay Area, by way of Saint Louis; all three of her sisters, Edith, Gloria, and Margaret, from Ohio, Los Angeles, and Atlanta; and her niece and nephews, Bonnie, Tony, and Ted, all walked out one by one, from behind a curtain. The look on Momma's face was priceless. I'd never seen her so happy in her life.

My sister later jokingly asked me, "What were you trying to do, give her a slow heart attack?" I joked back, "Well there were at least two or three medical professionals there, so she would have been in good hands." With few exceptions, everyone who was significant in my mother's and my life, was in attendance—and they were all there to honor my mother. Each person contributed to that wonderful night. There were so many heartfelt tributes and surprises, which I will hold in my heart forever. Her sisters and her best friends had everyone in stitches with laughter, reminiscing about the mischief they got into while growing up in Tuskegee, Alabama, and in their young adult years away from home.

The only thing that could have made it better is if I would have invited Tony. After going back and forth in my mind about it, against my better judgment, I decided not to. I'd only met him one month prior. I figured he wouldn't be around too long, so I didn't want to bother introducing him to my family, and then to have to answer the question once it didn't work out, "What happened to that guy at your mother's party?" If I knew then what I know now, that he'd be here twenty years later, he would have been right there with me amid my closest friends and family. Still, it was a wonderful time—we laughed, cried happy tears, and enjoyed each other's company all evening. Everything seemed to fall into place, the comradery among us was perfect.

Leading up to the day of the party, I remember trying to think of what I'd say to honor my mother. I couldn't get past the first few words without my eyes welling up with tears. This was the biggest thing that I'd ever done for her, or for anyone. And it was likely the biggest thing anyone else had ever done for her.

The trouble we had over the years didn't amount to all that she meant to me, or all that she had done for me, despite our many difficulties. She was my biggest fan; and in her own way she showed me how proud she was of me, and how much she dearly loved me.

One of my favorite verses in the Bible, Romans 8:28, was so fitting for this occasion: "*…all things work together for good to them that love God…*"

Success Principle Fourteen—Healing from Love Abuse

Many individuals suffer from emotional pain inflicted upon them from someone they believed was supposed to love them. But there is a stigma which exists around getting professional help, especially among people of color. Many feel that seeking therapy means that they are crazy. Nothing could be further from the truth. Rather, it means you care enough about yourself to invest in your mental and emotional well-being.

The only difference in our mental well-being and our physical well-being, is that you cannot see or feel emotional pain the same way you can see and feel physical pain. But without the proper attention, they can both lead to death.

Just as it is okay to consult with a physician about a nagging back pain, an ear ache, or chest pains, it is equally okay to speak with a mental health professional about fears, heartaches, and grief. The time and money spent on either is a personal investment that leads to a high quality of life.

Success Tips

❖ It is much more likely to effectively heal from emotional hurts with professional help, than it is to try to heal on your own.

❖ With competent counseling, it is less likely to repeat the same destructive habits and behaviors which led to the pain.

❖ Properly healing from emotional wounds has a positive impact on the hurting person's other relationships, i.e. with their children, friends, and coworkers—as it is said, *hurting people, hurt people.*

"It is the wise individual who makes up his mind that life is not going to be all sunshine, that all is not going to be perpetual pleasures."

—Booker T. Washington

What I've Learned from my Great-Grandfather's life

Even when life is at its best, usually there are clouds, rain, or a storm looming. I find that it is best to prepare for the bad days, during the good times, when I am emotionally strong. Every day that I wake up, I believe it is just another opportunity to get it right.

Fifteen
A Shift in the Atmosphere

The month following my mother's party, my daughter and I were ready to set sail. We were leaving for a Caribbean cruise to Barbados, Martinique, St. Thomas, and St. Lucia. I'd known Tony for about six weeks, and we were going out frequently. He was really turning out to be a change from the men I was used to. I knew he had a genuine interest in me when he gave me both his cell number and his home number. He also invited me to all of his basketball games for the league he played on. Above all else, he was a real gentleman. He was always polite; always on time; when we went out on dates he greeted me with roses; he always held doors open for me, and opened my car door; and he offered me his jacket when I was cold. He was very respectful, and he wouldn't even curse around me.

The evening before Regarah and I were to leave on the cruise I invited him over for pizza. This was the first time I'd ever allowed anyone since Vernon to meet one of my children. While I was out picking up the pizza Tony knocked on the door, and when Regarah told him I would be right back and invited him in per my instructions, he said, "Are you sure that's okay?" Even she, at 13-years-old, was impressed with his manners. I was impressed with them too.

At the door when he was leaving, knowing I'd be gone for the next eight days, we had our first kiss. Brief as it was, it was very intimate, and he stated, "Now you're making me not want to leave." The feeling was mutual. The kiss was just enough to keep our minds on one another while I was away. Waiting six weeks to kiss was definitely a first for me. Usually, before the first date ended, I had to pry hands off.

We started dating and began a serious relationship. Tony genuinely enjoyed my company, and it showed. We went out one night and I ran into an old friend and her husband, Gabriele and Cranston. I always admired "Gabby," ever since another friend, Charmaine, introduced us when Charmaine and I were attending the College of Alameda together. Although I felt somewhat intimidated by Gabby's allure and her natural elegance, there was something about her that was always warm and inviting. In addition, Gabby and Cranston were smart, sophisticated, and accomplished. When they immediately approved of Tony, for me that said a lot. That night we all began a close friendship. We did a lot together, including frequently going out for dinner and dancing; going on weekend camping and ski trips; and even taking a few Caribbean cruises.

One significant difference between Tony and my other relationships was that he didn't believe in going out to parties or clubs unless we were together. That was a welcome change, and actually a turn on. After he and I had been together for a while, I couldn't help but wonder if this was an intervention from God in response to the wish I shared with my daughter about meeting someone special: "...someone who likes to travel and do things with me; and it would be fine if he has a daughter too."

Not only did he have a beautiful little girl, but Tony loved to travel…and worked for United Airlines, so we could travel for next to nothing. The Scripture about God doing exceedingly, abundantly, over anything we could ever ask or imagine, comes to mind.

One night Tony invited me to see the beautiful night view of the Bay Area from his place in the Oakland Hills. His roommate was gone for the weekend. I just knew that was a ploy to get me in his bed. But after showing me around, we sat down and listened to some music and talked for a little while, and then we left to go on a date. For me, sadly, this was unheard of. *He was not normal,* I thought. But it was nice. It was definitely different. Someone enjoyed me for me, not what was underneath my clothes, but for what was deeper than that.

After Regarah and I returned from the cruise, it was another six weeks before he made additional moves. To be honest, I initiated the moves because I was beginning to think that either something was wrong with me or something was wrong with him. How could he wine and dine me, buy me flowers, take me with him to his basketball games, come over and watch television, talk and laugh, and then go home? I had always longed for this kind of attention… so why was I questioning it? I still had my work cut out for me.

Our upbringings were so completely different. Tony grew up in a small rural community in Laurinburg, North Carolina, in a nurturing home with both of his parents and two younger sisters. Most of the residents on his block were relatives, including his grandmother, aunts, uncles, and cousins. His father grew fresh vegetables in the backyard. His mother cooked nice Sunday dinners. He not only had home-cooked meals at home, but he had them up and down the block. He was raised in, and active in their church. The discipline instilled in him while he was in the Air Force, only added to his appeal. Tony was not the type of guy I would have given the time of day to in my past. He was too decent. He didn't have that edge or dysfunction that I was previously attracted to.

From the day I met Tony, I cut down on drinking because he became my "drug of choice." Since my relationship with him was going so well, I decided to stop going to counseling. When I let the counselor know that I wouldn't be coming back, she responded, "I'm concerned that with all you have been through, you may be stopping too soon." I underestimated and minimized in my mind what I'd been through. Still, her words reminded me of something another counselor said, "You didn't get this way overnight, and you can't expect to heal overnight." She was right. I was expecting over thirty years of damage and build up to dissipate now that I met Tony. Little did Tony or I know, he was beginning to fall deeply in love with someone who still had some unresolved issues.

As time went on Tony and I were inseparable. I remember thinking that we were moving too fast, and I told him that maybe we should take a break. He replied, "The only break I need from you is when I'm at work." I liked that response, and I never mentioned taking a break again. About a year into the relationship, we decided it probably would make more sense to live together and cut costs… so he moved in with me.

When my birthday rolled around Tony gave me a surprise dinner party on a rented yacht. He invited just four other couples who we were close to. I'd never had anyone give me a party, not even when I was growing up. As we cruised the San Francisco Bay, the guys crooned the ladies, imitating the Temptations, and other groups. We had an amazing time.

The next day, when I found out how much he'd spent on the party, the unhealed part of me reared its ugly head. I was livid. We were doing okay financially, but we were far from being wealthy, which the price of the entire party would have indicated. I could not believe he'd made that kind of decision. That was his introduction to another side of me. Although I felt it was not good sound judgment on his part, I later regretted that I made him feel bad about such a kind and thoughtful gesture. My initial harsh reaction was just the first of many more to come.

We got through that and three months later, in May, he proposed. Earlier in the day he'd said that he wanted to go out. When I said I was a little tired, he was obviously disappointed and he said it was important. I knew then what was about to happen. I blew what could have been a very pleasant and romantic surprise. We went to the lounge at the top of the Fairmont Hotel in San Francisco. After we ordered something to eat, he handed me a small heart-shaped box and asked me to marry him. I'd always wanted to know what it would feel like to have someone marry me for me, and not because we had a child. I said yes, and silently wished I had cooperated initially.

There would be many other times that I'd wished I'd cooperated a little better. Tony was always very patient with me. I kept wondering when his patience was going to run out. Perhaps I was unconsciously trying to sabotage the relationship. Maybe I thought I didn't deserve to be treated so well. Or, maybe my fear of abandonment was driving my reactions…trying to make him leave me before he left me on his own. It seemed every time I would think he was going to stop being so nice, he'd do something else nice. One day while having casual conversation, I said, "I'd like to go to New York over the Memorial Day weekend." The next thing I knew, he arranged a trip to New York, booking a hotel next door to the World Trade Center. We boarded the plane and because of his employee benefits, we flew first class. It was a nice date, and this time I didn't complain about the money.

During this period, I was excited about my upcoming graduation ceremony from Saint Mary's College. I will never forget how incredibly elated I was from the moment I woke up on graduation morning. Tony, Regarah, and I were getting dressed, and my excitement transpired onto them. Although I don't wish adversity on anyone, somehow, the barriers I had to overcome, made this accomplishment feel that much better.

After I put my graduation robe on, "This is how we do it," by Montel Jordan came on the radio. We danced and sang, and danced and sang some more. Now every time that song comes on the radio, it brings back a memory of that morning in my apartment in Alameda. At the graduation I'd never seen Momma so proud of me. My life didn't fall into place in quite the order she'd hoped, but it was falling into place, nonetheless.

While at PG&E, they paid for my bachelor's degree from Saint Mary's College. After receiving my bachelor's degree, my director, Michael Alexander, said, "What do you want to do now?" Remembering how much I liked working with people when I was at the bank, I told him I'd like to work directly with customers. He explained the only way to do that in a management position, would be as an account representative. Followed by, "I have a few connections if that is something you'd be interested in." Hesitantly, I asked him, "Would you be willing to do that for me?" I was performing well in his department, and I wasn't used to bosses letting good workers go. His answer was something I have never forgotten since. He said, in a very supportive manner, "If PG&E's president died tomorrow, do you think the company would fold?" In other words, his department would manage without me. He kept his word and I got into a position which was not easy to come by. I later secured a couple of positions that coworkers said I wouldn't get. I stayed at PG&E for sixteen years before leaving the company to pursue other opportunities.

During this time, Tony's daughter, Iesha, who her loved ones call, Esha, came back from his parents in North Carolina. I found out then that Esha's mother took her to North Carolina and left her with Tony's parents out of vengeance because she and Tony were not getting along. She was now 3-years-old, and living back with her mother, about thirty minutes away from us. Once Tony's daughter returned to California, he began going through a lot of drama with her mother. Without any forewarning, she abruptly removed their daughter from the day care that he was paying for.

Tony only found out his daughter was no longer at the daycare when he went to pick her up for his weekend visit, and she was not there. After that, the mother threatened to take her to Texas, vowing to never let him see her again. Iesha was the apple of Tony's eye. She was his heart. I now realized why he talked to me about his daughter the first night I met him. He was hoping to gain full custody of her all along. Tony was Iesha's heart as well. She would cry every time he dropped her off with her mother. It was as if she knew that she would be better off with him. I was always struck by just how much she loved and adored him. I guess because of my broken relationship with my father, it was hard for me to conceive of other little girls holding their fathers in such high esteem.

One evening when Tony took Iesha home, her mother and her boyfriend were drunk. They were fighting verbally and physically on the front lawn. Tony drove his daughter straight to the nearest police station to advise them of the court order and to tell them that he was not going to leave her in that environment. They agreed that he was doing the right thing.

The next morning, we went to the court to get a temporary custody order. We then found an attorney who, just because she was an attorney, did nothing more than intimidate Iesha's mother. We did most of the work ourselves. We did our homework and made the case for the attorney to present to the judge. This attorney had doubts all along that Tony could win, stating to him, "It's rare for a father to win custody from the mother in the state of California." We realized from her comments that Tony was basically on his own. I suggested that we call a church and find out how they might offer additional help. I thought of Allen Temple Baptist Church, a mega church in East Oakland. They had a large presence, and were known for the abundance of assistance they gave to African-Americans in the community.

Ironically, when I lived in Tassafaronga Village I used to pass Allen Temple on my way to the bus stop almost every day. I would think I was not good enough to go in there. I was a teenage mother and a welfare recipient living in the projects. I was somewhat intimidated about this church because of all that I'd heard about the prominence of the members; and how the pastor was one of Ebony Magazine's most famous preachers. Among their members were the chief of police, Black CEOs, doctors, lawyers, and local politicians and policymakers. These were the very people I always felt small around. Reluctantly I called…we were desperate.

Someone at the church put us in touch with one of the ministers, Reverend Donald Miller, who prayed with us over the phone. Not realizing the power of prayer at the time, I felt the attorney may have been right about a father's weak chance of gaining custody. Before Tony's court appearance, the temporary custody order was lifted, and he had to take Iesha back to her mother. When he dropped her off she had toys in her hand that he'd bought for her. Her mother snatched them from her tiny hands, and threw them at the car as Tony took off.

Not long after that, not only did Tony win full custody, but the mother's visits had to be supervised. He had her served with papers on the day he went to pick Esha up; and with the police there, Tony arranged for one of their mutual friends to take his daughter out of the home. Her mother was hysterical.

After a couple of days went by, and the mother calmed down, her only instruction for me was to make sure to wash her daughter's hair every day. However, I was not a hair person, not having to do much more with my hair other than wash and go, and yet, she expected me to wash her daughter's hair every day…and she was serious. Much to my satisfaction, Regarah had recently learned to do her own hair.

Caring for Esha's grooming and hygiene were two things that I couldn't take away from her mother. Before Tony gained custody, whenever he brought Esha to our house, she was always sparkling clean and neat from head to toe. Even so, after having totally neglected her daughter's emotional well-being, I couldn't get over the fact that she wanted to wash her long, thick, beautiful locks of hair, every day. While good hygiene and appearance are important,

I've seen too many mothers rest here, ignoring all of the other areas that need attention for a child to thrive and grow into a healthy adult—emotional, social, psychological, and intellectual areas. For a long time, I was certainly guilty of not appropriately providing in these areas for my children.

Winning custody was going to entail a much bigger adjustment than I had anticipated. Esha would be sharing a room with Regarah, who was ten years older than she was; they would have adjustment difficulties and challenges getting along; suddenly, for the first time in thirteen years, Regarah was not the youngest in the home; we'd have to put Esha in preschool; our expenses would increase; and I would have to share Tony's affections with her, not just every other weekend, but 24/7. I was torn between this beautiful little girl that I wished for, and having to share the affections of my fiancé with her.

To my surprise, Tony did his daughter's hair beautifully, even though it took him over an hour. Everyone thought I did it and they complimented me. I wanted to take the credit, but reluctantly I would tell the truth.

One Sunday we decided we'd visit Allen Temple Baptist Church and find out who Reverend Miller was so we could thank him personally for his prayers, and let him know the outcome of the case. We went to the 8:00 a.m. service. It was packed with churchgoers.

Ironically, or by Divine order, a portrait of my great-grandfather, Booker T. Washington, was painted in one of the stained glass windows. He is among other prominent black leaders such as Martin Luther King, Jr., Mary McCloud Bethune, Marian Anderson, George Washington Carver and Howard Thurman; out of those five, the only one my mother did not know on a personal level was Martin Luther King, Jr.

As the choir and clergy marched in, we wondered which one may have been Reverend Miller. When the service was over, one of the minsters pointed him out to us. We explained who we were, let him know the outcome of the case, and we thanked him. Little did we know how many more times he'd be involved in our lives.

Reverend Miller married us; he did the eulogy at my mother's memorial service; he was there to advise me when my daughter was placed on an involuntary 72-hour hold; he surfaced in a hospital parking lot, seemingly out of nowhere, when I was nervously going to visit Little Mario in ICU immediately following a motorcycle accident; he surfaced again when I was visiting a close friend of mine in ICU for a similar accident; he appeared again in the Christian bookstore when I was searching for a card for an inmate who was dating my daughter, and he wisely advised me not to do it; and he even surfaced early one Sunday morning as he was evangelizing outside of the Oakland Coliseum prior to a Raider game, and Tony and I were foregoing church to go to my very first tailgate party. *That was awkward. I'm sure he prayed for us that day.*

In the parking lot after church, two deacons—Deacon Harvell and Deacon Rhodes, stopped us to ask how we enjoyed the service. During the conversation, they discovered that, like Tony, they were all from the Carolinas. These two deacons defied the myth I'd heard for so long, that Allen Temple members were snobby. They encouraged us to come back. And we did…and we stayed. We started taking the girls as well. On several occasions my mother came with us. She and Reverend Miller became pretty good friends. She would tease him because he was a Cowboys fan and she traded in the Oakland Raiders for the San Francisco 49ers.

One Sunday when we were sitting way in the back of the church, during the invitation, Regarah was stirred up. She pleaded with me to take her up so she could accept the invitation. We scooted past all the people in the pew…Tony was right behind us. That day the three of us accepted the invitation and we were all baptized together. When Esha was older, she was baptized there, as well.

I prayed to God, telling Him that, like a sponge, I wanted to learn and absorb everything I could about the Father, the Son, and the

Holy Spirit. I didn't want to just react for the sake of reacting, but I wanted my spirit to be stirred, and I wanted to feel what others felt when they raised their hands, stomped their feet, and shouted, "Hallelujah." He answered that prayer too.

I soon met an angel of a friend at church, Mary Ellen. I don't even remember how or when exactly we met, I just know it happened and it changed my life. She and her husband Gerald playfully adopted us as their surrogate children. Often, I would look at Mary Ellen as she sat with her beautiful daughter and she'd gently caress her back and shoulders. I admired that, and I'd think how nice it must be to have your mother with you in church showering you with affection. I know my mother loved me a lot, but to see that kind of open affection really touched me deeply.

Next there was Mary Morris, my Sunday school teacher. She had a class that was the size of a small church. This was my first time ever attending Sunday school. She was a no-nonsense, in your face type of teacher who was not ashamed of the gospel. And though she fussed often, she loved even more. She knew your name, remembered your circumstances, and she would be there if you needed her. I guess I was stronger than I thought because you had to be strong to sit under her teachings. At the end of the class we'd stand in a large circle and request prayer, give praise reports, and then pray. There were over 100 people in the circle on any given Sunday.

After about three months I decided that maybe this class was too big and I went to a smaller class; but after two weeks I decided to go back to Mary's class. During the prayer circle she saw me in the distance, and she said, "You've been gone, I'm glad to see you back." Our bond grew, and she added more to my life than any other single person ever did. When she passed away, I was overwhelmed with grief. Because she knew that so many of her students loved her dearly, she'd often give us a reminder, saying, "I am just a mortal human being in a temporary body, so don't worship me, worship God."

There were several other angels that I met at this church, too many to name. I believe that before God allowed me to be introduced to the not-so-nice, He built a strong foundation under me so that I would not falter. God beautifully orchestrated this. My husband tried to warn me that there were also not-so-nice Christians and/or church goers. As a new member, I refused to believe there were bad people in church. I recall one visiting pastor, the renowned C.A.W. Clarke, from Dallas, saying, "Imagine what the bad people would be like if they weren't in church…and just think of how much better the good people, who don't go to church, would be if they did." In the beginning I had to constantly remind myself of this whenever I thought about fleeing the church. Besides that, there are good and bad people everywhere—concerts, the movies, at the park, in the mall, etcetera; but we don't stop going to those places.

When Momma died, most of my Sunday school class came to her service. This is when I found out how wonderful it is to belong to a church. Deaconesses brought food to my house. Deacons came and prayed with us. It was good, even though it was a sad occasion. To put it mildly, my church has become my pillar of strength and support.

I don't know how I made it for so many years without a church home and a relationship with God. I'm convinced that even when I didn't know it—when my parents weren't a source of stability for me, and when I lived in the projects and finished high school—He was protecting and leading me all along.

As my life continued to improve, I began to realize that the God I'd thought I'd known was real and that He was a good God who brought me through when I didn't even know He was there. For the first time in my life, I realized it was not about religion, but rather a relationship with God; and then my spirituality began to flourish and the rest is history. All things began to work together…

Even with my new and improved perspective on life, and my new found spirituality, I still lacked a feeling of wholeness. Thus, the adjustment of a new little one in the home, as adorable as she was, proved to be overly taxing. Perhaps there was jealousy on my part as far as Tony's daughter's intrusion into my union with her father. He now had to divide his attention. It was obvious that he planned on being the best father that he could be. He loved his daughter. But hadn't I wished for this? I suppose my prayer was not specific enough. I said I wish for a good man with a daughter, but I neglected to elaborate on what kind of mother she should have.

Unbeknownst to our new little addition, Esha, I was far from where I used to be, but not where I needed to be, in terms of emotional healing. Esha was an innocent child entering into the home of a woman whose father had abandoned her; who never knew what it was like to have a full-time father; and who had major difficulties raising her two children without fathers. I had father issues big time. No one was really prepared or in touch with my sense of weakness and my need to be in control of my frail little world, as it was.

Amazingly Esha knew where she wanted to be, or rather who she wanted to be with. It didn't matter where he was, as long as she could be with her father. There was an air about her that never took being with him for granted. From the time I first met her, she displayed a certain gratefulness. Perhaps it was because her mother left her 3,000 miles away with his parents when she was just six-months-old. Perhaps it was because of the outings and the trips he took her on, from his weekly softball games to the North Pole in Alaska to see Santa and his real live reindeers when she was a toddler.

Whatever it was, she chose to plant herself in it and enjoy it. Since she was six months old, she'd never really had a home. She had been transported to her grandparents in North Carolina and then living in so many different places with her unstable mother—moving from relatives to friends, to boyfriends' homes; and then staying with her father every other weekend.

When Iesha was four-years-old we enrolled her in preschool. With Tony having to work, I was the only one who could take her for her preschool physical. We had recently learned from her mother that she had none of her shots. Unlike when my son pushed the screw up his nostril nearly twenty years ago, at least this time a nurse would be present during my anxiety. Still, I considered it a cruel test I'd have to pass.

Initially Iesha was excited about going to the doctor, and her excitement was another thing about her that baffled me. She was unlike any kid I'd ever known, especially my two. She got a thrill from going to the doctor. But that quickly changed when the needles came out. She was paranoid. We just had to get through this series of at least five different shots to catch up on the minimum immunizations. They had to bring in an additional nurse, and the two of us had to hold her down as she screamed and squirmed, and a second nurse gave her all of her shots. The thought, sight, or sound, of anyone physically hurting children agonizes me. Even if it's, as it was in this case, for their own good. To calm Esha down, I promised her that I would buy her anything she wanted from the toy store on our way home. That worked for a little while.

As we drove home after the traumatic experience, she spotted the Toys R Us marquee in front of the store. She immediately reminded me of my promise. So we turned into the parking lot and went into this enormous store, which I'd imagined to a child 4-years-old appeared ten times the actual size. After we looked around the store, she'd made her selection. To my dismay, once again, she baffled me. She selected a very practical plastic yellow umbrella. And to my further dismay, she kept that umbrella for about four years without losing it or leaving it anywhere. She was so completely opposite of most kids I'd encountered.

Unfortunately, there was a gradual sort of resentment building up inside of me as I compared Tony and his daughter, and their relationship, to me and my children, and our relationship. I dubbed them both, "Goodie two shoes." It felt to me that they thought they were better than us. The gradual resentment led to verbal arguments that were about much more than what appeared on the surface. Still expecting that a man would make me whole, I hadn't done all of my work in therapy. Again, I was reminded of the counselor's words, "You didn't get this way overnight, and you can't expect to heal overnight."

I began to place Tony on a pedestal as I compared his life to mine. According to him, he'd never even put a joint to his lips. He'd never cut school. He addressed his elders, "Yes ma'am," and "No sir." His parents adored him. Placing him on a pedestal was dangerous because when people are placed on pedestals there's nowhere for them to go but down. In the beginning I think Tony was shocked at some of the words that would come out of my mouth. He had no idea of my past, with and without my father; my fights with my brother; and the emotional and physical abuse of my previous relationships. He had no idea.

I found a new counselor, and I started going to therapy again. Momma was even proud to hear this. I remember her commenting, "I know Tony is glad." I never knew she felt that way until she said that. Counseling helped so much that it led me to graduate school to become a counselor myself. While returning to counseling helped tremendously, there was still a lingering feeling that something was lacking internally for me. I began praying daily for wholeness.

Soon after Esha came to live with us, we decided to go find out what we'd have to do to qualify to buy a home. Our number one requirement was that we both wanted to live where the schools were decent. House shopping proved to be an interesting experience. One realtor who was showing homes in a new development in Alameda, without asking anything about our occupations or incomes, told us outright that we could not afford the homes.

Others weren't quite as forward, but you could tell they weren't interested in entertaining the possibility of us moving in the neighborhood. Once we qualified for the home we bought, we knew that we could have afforded many of the others we were turned away from.

Our lot was under construction. Our future home would be a four-bedroom, three full bath, single-family home, complete with a sun window in the kitchen, high ceilings, and skylights. Although the real estate agent referred to our dwelling as a starter home, I never would have imagined that from where I'd come, I would actually have a home where I could pick out the flooring, carpet, tile and cabinetry. It felt good to provide each of the girls with not only their own rooms, but their own shared bathroom as well. It was especially nice to provide a home for Esha, who'd been shuffled around for most of her young life.

We moved into our brand new home in August. Often, I would look down from the upstairs balcony overlooking the entryway and the living and dining room, and I'd thank God as I wondered what could have instilled in me the perseverance to go from where I started, to here.

In October, my father passed away. He was 83-years-old. He had several complications, mainly from the hard drinking he'd done for most of his life. Though I was sad, I can't say that I was heavily grieved. I was sad more about the fact that he cut our relationship short, than I was about him passing away. Still, I forgive him, and I cherish the good memories that I have of him, no matter how short-lived they were. There are several which will remain in my heart forever.

Tony and I were growing in our spirituality and the guilt of living together out of wedlock, and setting this kind of example for our children began to weigh heavily on us. After moving in, and getting the girls settled in their respective schools, we set a date to get married in March of the next year, in our new home. We asked Reverend Miller to officiate the wedding. We had no furniture and I wanted to invite 150 guests. During our premarital counseling, Reverend Miller, who doubted we could comfortably fit that many people in our living and dining space, jokingly told Tony to just say "Yes dear." In fact, he told us that the key to his over 25 years of marriage to his wife, was as simple as those two words, "Yes dear." I was good with that piece of advice. And as far as fitting all the guests in the house, my motto was, "Where there's a will, there's a way."

We did have to attach a large white party tent to the back of our home, but it worked. Not only did we accommodate 150 people comfortably, but we had an overflow, as many of my relatives who I hadn't seen in years before my father's funeral, came to celebrate with us. And everyone was happy. While my friend and wedding coordinator, Charla, my bridesmaids, Vickie, Regarah, and Gabby, and my maid of honor, Carmen, tended to me upstairs in my room, I glimpsed out of the window. There was a trail of guests walking toward my house. Among them were many of my relatives on my father's side of the family who came from Los Angeles, Inglewood, and Pasadena. A tear dropped from my eye as I thought, *they all came for me…to share in my special day.* I was overcome with joy.

Everyone who was special in my life played an important part that day, including my wonderful in-laws who came from North Carolina, my brother, James, who was a groomsman, my son Mario, who gave me away, and my daughter, Esha, who was the flower girl. My proud mother, who was absolutely glowing on that day, handed me a bracelet, and said, "Sarah, in the tradition of giving the bride something old, something new, something borrowed, something blue, here is something old." It was the most beautiful antique looking bracelet adorned with purple amethyst stones. That is my birthstone. Sadly, after my mother passed away, years later someone robbed our house and took my bracelet. Out of everything else they took and/or destroyed—computers, cameras, televisions, money—the bracelet was the only thing I cared about.

When we said our vows, Reverend Miller included our three children, Mario, Regarah, and Iesha. After we all said our "I do's" at first you could hear a pin drop, and then you heard the sniffles around the room. On my wedding day, everything fell into place, as if divinely ordered.

The emcee for our reception was a well-known radio personality in the Bay Area, Timothy Alexander White. But that wasn't why I chose him. He was actually one of the customers from Crocker Bank who would wait on me to help him. The last time he came to my window was the day he got the position as a DJ on KSOL, a popular R & B station in the Bay Area.

After our reception, Tony and I left for our honeymoon in Negril, Jamaica. Afterwards, we went to our second reception hosted by his parents, in Laurinburg, North Carolina. I fell in love with Laurinburg and McKenzie Street, the block where my in-laws live, and where my husband grew up. My favorite part was sitting on the porch with his family while it rained in the hot humid air. I never witnessed rain like that in California.

It wasn't uncommon that I'd never heard of Tony's hometown. There are only about 16,000 residents in the entire 12.6 square mile area of the city, compared to over 400,000 residents in the 78 square mile city of Oakland, where I grew up. There wasn't much to do when we went there, so Tony would always take me by a few landmarks. One of them was Laurinburg Institute, one of the only remaining private Black boarding schools in the country. Ironically, we later found out that Booker T. Washington traveled to Laurinburg along with Spike Lee's great-grandfather, William J. Edwards, an educator and graduate of Tuskegee, to survey the education needs of the Black children; after which, my great-grand-father sent two of his Tuskegee graduates, Emmanuel Monty and Tinny McDuffie, to begin the school in 1904.

When I first started to study the Bible, I remember wondering and worrying about what God thought about me divorcing and being in a second marriage. In the handful of times that I believe I have heard audibly from God, this was one of them. In a dream an authoritative voice came to me that said, "You made the first marriage, but I made this one." That was confirmation for me that my marriage was divinely ordered. However, not without ups and downs. I can't count how often I have had to remind myself of that dream. Our marriage is not perfect or problem free, but we handle our issues differently now. When problems arise we do the hard work that it takes to maintain a healthy marriage—including, marriage counseling, reading material about how to keep going when the going gets tough, attending couple's workshops, and of course, prayer, and reading the Bible.

Counseling helped me find a man who would treat me well. Church led me to a relationship with God. I had come a long way, I'd overcome many obstacles, and my life was definitely looking up. Yet, I was still unable to shake the feeling that something in my life was missing.

Success Principle Fifteen—Making Marriage Work

Marriage involves integrating each person's own paradigm and view of the world into the union. This probably sounds a lot easier than it actually is. Because the development of personality is so complex, and our minds are so intricately organized, complications are inevitable. The chances of combining our thoughts and wishes; our ideas and ideals; and our principles and values, going off without a hitch—is rare indeed.

Infatuation is usually the beginning of most intimate relationships. This is a normal phase. It is also normal for this phase to taper off. In tapering off, one or both people in the relationship will begin to see the flaws of the other. As the infatuation continues to dissipate, it is common for each person, mostly unconsciously, to want the other person to stop and save them.

If the love is genuine, and the integration of the two paradigms and views of the world is done well, it creates a happy marriage. If the integration is done poorly, no matter how much love there is between the couple, it can wreak havoc.

Success Tips

❖ Marriage, like all relationships, takes ongoing work to be successful—even as much as keeping up with reading material on what makes a happy marriage and then implementing the recommendations, can make a big difference.

❖ While weddings are quite meaningful, we often mistakenly focus too much attention on having a memorable wedding, and too little attention on having a happy marriage.

❖ It is vitally important that each person realizes that a fifty-fifty proposition in the marriage is not enough—each must be willing to give one hundred percent of themselves in order for the relationship to thrive.

"The individual who puts the most into life is the one who gets the most out of life."

—Booker T. Washington

What I've Learned from my Great-Grandfather's life

I shouldn't judge others by their skin color, social status, or political party, but rather by their heart. There is good and bad in all of us. It is our heart that determines if good or bad will be our driving force. I strive for my heart to be better today than yesterday, and even better tomorrow than today.

Sixteen

Lifting the Veil

One would wonder, with all the richness of our heritage and all the greatness of our heirs, why this branch of the Booker T. Washington family tree was so dysfunctional. Perhaps my mother's father, who she adored, dying when she was just 19-years-old played some part. That coupled with the fact that she didn't believe my father really loved her, but married her only for her name could be another reason. And then there was the infamous 1960s when other Blacks likened my great-grandfather's non-confrontational philosophies to those of a sell-out. Whatever it was, you can't give what you don't have. Thus, a generational curse spiraled down to my generation. We didn't know where we came from, and we were in constant conflict about where we were going.

Needless to say, with everything I went through in my life, and with everything my children went through while they were growing up, we were all bound to have a tough time. We didn't understand all of the things that we were up against…we had not even a clue. I had to wonder if the cycle that started with my mother, then passed down to me, would ever end. Before it got better, it seemed to become progressively worse with every passing day. But then one day something happened that would point to a brighter future, and inevitably turn all of our lives around. It was the missing piece of the puzzle I'd been searching for.

In 1996 two of my cousins, Ricky and Chuck, came up with a brilliant idea. They decided to host the first ever Booker T. Washington family reunion so that our children could know their legacy. My mother, our two daughters, Tony, and I flew out of Oakland airport into Atlanta. We rented a car, and then drove two hours to Tuskegee.

When we arrived on the campus of Tuskegee University, there were news reporters, journalists, community leaders, students, and faculty crowded all around. They were all waiting to welcome the Washington family to Tuskegee. The mayor was also there, and community residents, including Lionel Ritchie's mother, Alberta Foster, who at one time lived next door to my mother and her sisters when they were all growing up across the street from the campus.

Still loving to provide a valuable service to people, I volunteered to work at the registration table. While sitting there registering family members, many people came over to me. I learned that they were awe-struck that his descendants were still alive. And I was awe-struck that they cared so much. They were inspired simply by our presence. They asked for autographs and interviews. They asked to take pictures with us. And some just wanted a chance to talk and get to know us. I was so amazed. They all knew what I didn't know about my famous family legacy. While I was joyfully doing my job, Momma came over to sit with me. Out of shock and curiosity, I turned to her, and asked, "Momma, what is this?" Before she could answer, someone else came over to talk to us. We never got back to the answer to that question.

I was enlightened by so much during those few days. I learned about the famous statue at the entrance of the campus. The sculpture is entitled, "Lifting the Veil." It was dedicated to Booker T, Washington after he died, by renowned sculptor Charles Keck in 1922. It portrays Booker T. Washington lifting a veil of ignorance off of a former slave's eyes, a topic my great-grandfather often addressed, stating, *"A race, like an individual, lifts itself up by lifting others up."* People from all over the world take pictures in front of that statue.

It took nearly twenty years after I graduated from high school to realize the significance of my lineage. It was at this reunion that I began to understand how important my great-grandfather's work was. On campus I was struck by the original buildings—built by hand, brick by brick, by Booker T. Washington and his students, all former slaves and their descendants—using bricks that they had made themselves. The bricks were of such superior quality that they sold them to fund the school. This was the students' first lesson in entrepreneurship.

After I returned home from my reunion, highly inspired, I set out to learn everything that I could about my history. I read my great-grandfather's bestselling autobiography, "Up from Slavery," for the first time. "Up from Slavery," was so inspirational that it was translated into over 17 different languages, and to this day, it has never been out of print. I studied other books, either written by, or written about my great-grandfather. I did research, and I asked questions.

During the course of learning about my family history, I discovered that I have fifteen cousins who are also the great-grandchildren of Booker T. Washington, and I am the last born. That meant, not only did I complete the fourth generation of Booker T. Washington, but more importantly, it meant...I was the 16th of Booker T. Washington's 16 great-grandchildren. The number sixteen, which always carried a measure of shame for me, due to having my son at the age of sixteen, turned around. This gave great new meaning to, "The whole is greater than the sum of its parts."

During the reunion, I realized I came from a great man, a man of God, a man of rare achievement. Though I was born well before we had the reunion in 1996, I didn't start living until then. Granted, I had evolved into a grown woman, yet I was like an infant trying to come into myself through many trials and tribulations. For many years I was going in the wrong direction, feeling confused, abandoned, and forsaken. I was trying to find my way, while discovering who and what I was, and what would make me happy.

Everything started happening around the same time—there would be no "Knight in shining armor" who would come and rescue me, but it was spiritual growth through church, emotional healing through counseling, and the awareness of my family history through our first family reunion, that changed my life. Finally, it was all beginning to make sense.

On the heels of learning my history, I wanted to help others who faced similar circumstances as the ones I faced. I enrolled in the graduate psychology program at John F. Kennedy University. Momma was well-pleased with me once again. As time went on, I delved deeper into our history. I began to carefully suggest to my mother that our family heritage was an honor and a privilege, not an *accident of birth*. Slowly her resistance to talk about her famous legacy began to lift. Whatever bleakness was still there began to turn into more of a humbleness in nature.

Right around that time Regarah graduated from high school. It had been kind of hit-or-miss leading up to that day, so we were all elated. I pulled Momma through the large crowd and we got to the very front row. That was our tradition, sitting front and center wherever we went to see Regarah do anything.

A couple days later, Momma asked me to come by. When I got there, at almost 80-years-old, she was in her office organizing files in her file cabinet. I was standing there waiting for her to tell me what she wanted, when she very kindly looked up at me and said, "I just wanted to see you." I thought that was so sweet, and I stayed a little longer, made small talk, and then I left.

More than ten years before, Momma finally got a break in life, and I'd never seen her more happy and content. When she first moved into this beautiful brand new building, and began her new position as the first manager there, she vowed she would be there until the end. She said they would have to take her out on a stretcher. She never asked for much in terms of material gain. In fact, she used to tease me when I told her she needed to come to church more, by responding, "As long as I know God is up there preparing a place for me, it doesn't matter what size it is."

Momma had aged gracefully. She'd stopped smoking, she began keeping her living space immaculate, and she was debt-free. Momma was genuinely happy. After months and months of her boss trying to coerce her, she finally agreed to step down from the manager position to become the activities director. That was hard for her, but she was getting up in age, so she reluctantly gave in.

She voluntarily didn't own a television. The only time she watched television for more than a few minutes, was when Princess Diana died. She also started watching Oprah occasionally after work in one of the tenant's units. When tenants passed away, the maintenance staff would give Momma the deceased person's television, and she always politely gave it to someone else. She continued to get lost in her reading, and though she cut down, she still enjoyed her cocktails.

Momma's mind was always sharp. She and I often had friendly debates about current affairs. She discussed football, basketball, and golf with my husband, like she was a sports commentator. But lately, Regarah and I noticed she was starting to forget things more often. That worried us because at nearly eighty-years-old, she was still a workaholic, and working was her livelihood. I didn't know what she'd do if she couldn't work anymore.

One day, while at work at PG&E, I got that call that I'd always dreaded. Terry, one of Momma's favorite people on the staff at Noble Tower, was on the other end of the phone. When he said hello, I could tell in his voice it wasn't good. I can't even quite remember how he told me Momma passed away. He was very close to my mother, and I am certain my response devastated him more than he already was. I let out a loud cry, and I cried and cried. A co-worker who was working nearby was also shaken.

I knew Momma wasn't well because I had accompanied her to a recent doctor's visit, and he told her she needed to begin dialysis. That, coupled with the forgetfulness, was not the way she wanted to live. Momma was just too independent to let anyone have to assist her to live in any way. But I never entertained the thought that she may not have long. I just couldn't conceive of my mother not being on this earth with me. It was as if she was supposed to live forever. I believe she gave up after hearing the latest news from her doctor.

When Terry found her lying unconscious on the floor of her apartment, it appeared that she was getting ready for work. After calling my sister Edith, and then calling Aunt Gloria and my cousin Bonnie, I went to Momma's apartment. When I arrived, I was unable to go up. I decided that I wanted to remember Momma the last way that I saw her when she was alive. James and Tony met me there, and while they went up to her unit, I just sat outside on the curb and cried some more. My biggest fan would no longer be there beaming at my accomplishments, or to make sure I got home safe and sound whenever she knew I was out at night, and especially if the weather was bad. I was truly going to miss her.

Momma always said throughout her life, "Give me my flowers while I'm alive." In other words, she wasn't concerned about having lots of frills when she was gone. So, I tried to give her that as much as possible while she was living. Still, when she passed away, we had a celebration of her life in my church. Reverend Miller gave the eulogy; her sorority sisters gave a traditional tribute; there was song and praise; one of the most beautiful voices in our church, Carolyn Anderson, sang "Wind Beneath my Wings." Regarah tearfully read a statement about her grandmother that brought everyone to joyful tears; my mother's three sisters were there; and the house was full.

Momma often said she wanted to be buried near her parents. That request was granted; today she lays to rest very close to her mother and father in the family cemetery on the campus of Tuskegee University. She is also among other great American leaders, including Booker T. Washington, George Washington Carver, and Olivia Davidson. I know Momma is well-pleased.

Mario honored his grandmother by deciding on his own to get his G.E.D. He has an associate's degree in heating, ventilating, and air conditioning, he owns a barber shop, and he has a thriving car sales business in Oakland. He broke the generational cycle of not having a father in his life. He adores and spends lots of time with his two children, Amari and Velez, and if it's at all possible, they adore him more.

Regarah is working in her passion as a licensed esthetician, surpassing national records in her craft. She plays the role of both mother and father to her only child, Saniya, whose father, Damont, unfortunately fell victim to Black on Black crime, when he was murdered on the streets of Oakland. Saniya was just 3-years-old at the time. Just before he was killed, he had come from the park with Saniya and Regarah. He was teaching Saniya how to ride her tricycle, and showing her how to play on the monkey bars. Saniya often asks Regarah to buy a balloon, and then they go to the park and let it go up in the air in honor of her father.

Esha, upon graduating from high school, and being accepted to a few different colleges, decided to go to Tuskegee. She graduated in May 2014 with a bachelor's degree in psychology. I can't begin to describe what it felt like to sit in the audience at her graduation, and look down at the hundreds of African-American great minds who were about to impart their knowledge throughout the country, armed with bachelor's, master's, and doctorate degrees. The thrill of my daughter being among them is indescribable.

I am proud to say that not one of our children became a teenage parent. Mario and Regarah were 25 and 26-years-old, respectively, before they became parents. Esha doesn't have any children yet. I am certain that my mother and my great-grandfather would be very proud of each of them, as they continue to grow, break negative cycles, and continue to strive higher.

I am also convinced that God purposely placed me in the blood-line of Booker T. Washington…not just to be, but to carry on his legacy of lifting those who struggle to lift themselves. When I think of how there are over 7 billion people in the world, and my great-grandfather only has sixteen great-grandchildren…and I am the last born—it defies all earthly explanation.

With all three of my children leading productive lives, I feel tremendously blessed. I have a peace of mind that I never thought was possible. Finally, a bridge between my deprivation and my reign has been revealed. My journey was by no means easy, but it has led to a place that I could have only arrived at with the trials I overcame along the way. It also allows me to have genuine compassion for the underprivileged, while affording me the wherewithal to empower them to do something about their circumstances. Where I am today is remarkably different from where I started, and it has been an incredible ride.

As God would have it, I found my voice, and I began delivering speeches across the country.

Success Principle Sixteen—The Head, the Hand, and the Heart Principle

Booker T. Washington's foundation for improving the lives of the masses of Blacks in the South who struggled to lift themselves up, was built on the "The head, hand, and heart" principle. For me personally, the head was the knowledge I learned about my history; the hand was the work I did through counseling; and the heart was my spiritual growth that started in the church.

The "head" involved book knowledge. When the school in Tuskegee first opened its doors many of the students were unable to read and write. His feeling was, as he explained it, "It is important and right that all privileges of law be ours, but it is vastly more important that we be prepared for the exercise of these privileges." So, one of his first orders of business, was to teach them how to read and write.

Next was the area of the "hand." This involved the hard work that it was going to take to improve their lives. Concerning work, he said, "We must not only become reliable, progressive, skillful, and intelligent, but we must keep the idea constantly before our youth that all forms of labor, whether with the head or the hand, are honorable." We mustn't magnify the work of the white collar worker at the expense of minimizing the work of the blue collar worker. They are both important and noble forms of earning a living, and creating a better quality of life.

Lastly, Booker T. Washington emphasized the role of the "heart." The heart involved the service we give back to others. He believed it was not enough to have an education and a high quality of life, for the sake of having them. But rather, it was for the sake of making someone else's life better.

Success Tips

❖ Never cease to grow, improve, explore, and learn something new—the head.

❖ Each day we wake up, presents another opportunity for us to work at getting it right—the hand.

❖ An effective way to find happiness, is to distract yourself from your problems by making someone else happy—the heart.

Endearing Moments

Tony, Sarah, Rev. Miller (March 29, 1997)

Mr. and Mrs. Anthony Rush receive a Senate Proclamation from cousin, Diane E. Watson, California State Senator (1978-1990 and 1994-1998 and 2001-2003) U.S. Ambassador to Micronesia, appointed by President Bill Clinton (1999-2003) U.S. Congresswoman (2003-2011)

Sarah's Sister, Edith

Cousins Bonnie and Robin (09/12/09)

Sarah with Cousin Amanda Washington standing in front of the White House at the Washington Family Reunion (July 2014).

Cousins Ricky and Chuck (09/12/09)

Booker T. Washington Statue at Hampton University.
He is the university's most notable alumni.

Sarah standing next to Olivia Davidson's photo in Tuskegee University Chapel (2010)

Sarah in front of Cousin Diane's Office in Congress (2010)

Sarah Signing Autograph (January 2005)

Sarah Speaking at St. Joseph Notre Dame High School (February 2011)

Brother James and His Son Tyler

Mario, Jr., Tony, Sarah, Regarah, Amari, Velez, Saniya (2014)

Booker T. Washington Family Reunion (2014) at the
White House with Secretary of Homeland Security, Jeh Johnson

Sarah Speaking at a Booker T. Washington Family Reunion
at Tuskegee University

Iesha's Tuskegee University Graduation (May 2014)

Afterword

We had been sold into slavery by Africans, we were made miserable in slavery at the hands of White people, we were loved through slavery by our own, and we were freed from slavery by the prompting of a White man. A whole other book would have to be written in order to capture and attempt to explain the downfall and confusion that has happened since then. Today, I consider us to be in a form of modern day slavery, for a combination of reasons—ourselves, systems, stigmas, and misfortune, to name a few.

The most important lesson that I have learned from my great grandfather about true freedom, and have incorporated into my life, is that education, personal responsibility, and character building, go a long way toward achieving success; and that within disadvantaged African-American communities there is a lot of untapped strength and potential to be uncovered and released.

Today, underprivileged African-American children say they don't have anyone to look up to. Many of them turn to gangs and other negative forces in order to feel inclusion, important, and respected. How can we condemn them? After all, everyone wants to feel these same elements. While others may join exclusive sororities and fraternities, these children get in where they fit in, even if that means joining a group of criminals.

The vast majority of African-Americans are descendants of someone who survived the middle passage from Africa to America. That alone is evidence of unparalleled strength in our blood. Imagine if more of us embrace that truth, and turn it into inspiring stories of our strength. We owe our courageous ancestors who laid a foundation for us, to do the same for the generations to come.

After working for a period in the field of psychotherapy, I decided that I was interested in empowering a greater number of individuals than I could in therapy. I especially desired to help underprivileged youth and their families, who had a strong desire to improve their lives, but who lacked the necessary skills, support, and resources to do so.

In doing that work, a few years ago I took a group of teens across the United States on a trip following in the footsteps of Booker T. Washington from slavery to freedom—from the plantation in Franklin County, Virginia, to Malden, West Virginia, where he and his family went when slavery ended; to Hampton, Virginia, where he received his formal education; to Washington, D.C., where he was the first Black, invited by Theodore Roosevelt, to dine in the White House, and to Tuskegee, Alabama, where Washington started a school so that former slaves and their descendants could receive an education, and improve their lives. Exposing youth to their history in this way is one of the most effective ways I can think of to carry on the legacy of my great-grandfather.

In Conclusion...

With the odds stacked against me for much of my life, I never thought I would be where I am today. My whole life has changed since that day on the campus of Tuskegee University, and making that connection to my great-grandfather. Upon claiming my heritage and revealing my lineage I've been referred to as "blue blood," "Black royalty," and "a living legacy," to name a few. People have purposely rubbed up against me, stating, "I want some of your heritage to rub off on me." While I don't take any of this for granted, I believe God placed me in this bloodline not just "to be," but rather, "to do."

Though I missed out on having a sweet sixteen birthday party, proms, homecomings, dances and other functions, I knew there was no question that I would finish school. I thank God that He allowed me to see both sides of life—the good and the not so good, the rich and the poor, the highly educated and the high school dropout. I allow myself to be taught by those who have everything, and those who have nothing. I am fulfilled by helping people who don't have anything; and I have compassion for those who don't have support or encouragement, but want more.

Without counseling, developing a relationship with God, an awareness of my history, and a village to see me through, none of this would have been possible.

Counseling

Having someone to listen to me who understood and did not judge my story, was a tremendous help. From there, I began to clean up all of the relationships in my life. It was a process that took some time to get right. I was also able to deal with my feelings about my parents and to forgive them. In the last several years of my mother's life we were very close and she'd become my best friend.

It is vital to our mental, psychological, and emotional well-being that we get away from the stigma connected with the terms, "mental health" and "clinical counseling." Too many among us suffer in silence, to avoid the ridicule of others once it is known that they are in counseling. It is common for people who are miserable, to make others miserable, giving truth to the saying, "Misery loves company." Allow yourself, and/or others to get the help they need. We will all be better in the long run.

Developing a Relationship With God

For me, it was never enough to just go to church, but I needed to seek and study the word of God, and have His word so deeply implanted in my heart and mind, that nothing could shake my faith. Then I was better able to follow His will for my life. Once we know the will of God, and practice it, though we will never be perfect and there will always be storms in our midst, we will weather them safer, much calmer, and with more peace.

Awareness of My History

Since 1996 when I attended the first ever Booker T. Washington family reunion in Tuskegee, Alabama, hardly a day goes by that I don't wake up and think about my great grandfather. The realization of who he was struck me like a lightning bolt. It was a whole new experience. I now had answers to my questions about my reason for being, about who I am, and about where my journey may take me.

With everything falling into place, I now have a platform on which to stand as a confident leader, advisor, counselor, educator, and author. My goals are clear and my purpose is evident. I realize that I have not come this far, facing and overcoming so many trials and tribulations, in vain.

Even with all that I have achieved, I consider myself an ongoing work in progress. Growing in all areas of my life, especially mentally, emotionally, physically and spiritually. As I make mistakes, I use every opportunity to learn from them and view them as stepping stones to a better me. If someone were to ask me for the ingredients to overcoming pains from the past and becoming happy and healing, I would say: A spiritual relationship with God; a counselor; a village, and knowing their history.

By telling my story, I hope to inspire and redirect others, especially young people, who may feel as I once did, lost and broken, without a clue about how to become whole.

Special Acknowledgements: Support From My Village

Our journey is meaningless if we don't have others to share in our successes. In addition to counseling, spiritual growth, and a new found awareness of my history, it helped for me to have a village of friends, family, and others who without judgment, believed in me. Past and present girlfriends like Vickie Reynold, Sherlyn Martin, Gabrielle Logan, Charla Edwards, Jacqueline Bautista, Carmen Stone, Deborah Jenkins, Yvonne DeSena, and Joyce Grant, and of course my "California Berries." I know that I can always count on each of these ladies for inspiration, encouragement, and sound advice. In their own way, they have given so freely of themselves... expecting nothing in return.

There are members of my family in my village, who continue to provide examples for me that I will carry for a lifetime. My cousins, Bonnie and Robin, each adoringly took me under their wings when I was just a little girl, and taught me by example how to be pretty and smart simultaneously; Ricky and Chuck initiated our very first Washington family reunion, providing a foundation for the work I do today; and my cousin Diane, with all of her warmth, shared many stories with me about my O'Neal/Slater bloodline, allowing me to see the bigger picture. My siblings, James and Edith, are always willing to put up with me, that says a lot, and they love me anyhow. My Aunt Gloria and my late Aunt Margaret, opened their hearts and their doors for me when I was a little girl, naturally setting examples of poise and elegance. Though I met my Aunt Edith later in life, I knew she set the bar high, and when she uttered the words, "I'm proud of you," after my mother passed away, it meant everything.

My village would not be complete without naming those who have gone from this earth, far too soon. I once heard Oprah Winfrey say, after she'd lost a loved one, "What did you come to teach me, that you had to die in order for me to learn?" From then on, whenever I lose someone in my village, I search for the lesson they came to teach me. Among my most recent instructors are, my late sister, Lynne Walters; Deacon Reggie Mastin; Elizabeth Chambers, Rose Calbert West, Irvin Davis, Jr.; and my granddaughter's father, Damont Brown. I trust you are all in a better place.

Sarah Washington O'Neal Rush's Lineage to her Great-Grandfather, Booker T. Washington

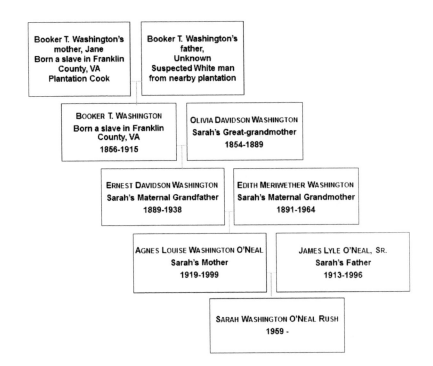

Appendix A

The Line of the Booker T. Washington Family Tree that Leads to Sarah Washington O'Neal Rush

Booker T. Washington had three children, Portia, Booker, and Ernest Davidson Washington. My Mother, Agnes Louise, was the first born of Ernest Davidson's and Edith Meriwether's four daughters. I was the last born of Agnes Louise and James Lyle O'Neal's children.

Appendix B

Booker T. Washington Delivers the 1895 Atlanta Exposition Address

On September 18, 1895, African-American spokesman and leader Booker T. Washington spoke before a predominantly white audience at the Cotton States and International Exposition in Atlanta. His "Atlanta Compromise" address, as it came to be called, was one of the most important and influential speeches in American history. Although the organizers of the exposition worried that "public sentiment was not prepared for such an advanced step," they decided that inviting a black speaker would impress Northern visitors with the evidence of racial progress in the South. Washington soothed his listeners' concerns about "uppity" blacks by claiming that his race would content itself with living "by the productions of our hands."

Mr. President and Gentlemen of the Board of Directors and Citizens:

One-third of the population of the South is of the Negro race. No enterprise seeking the material, civil, or moral welfare of this section can disregard this element of our population and reach the highest success. I but convey to you, Mr. President and Directors, the sentiment of the masses of my race when I say that in no way have the value and manhood of the American Negro been more fittingly and generously recognized than by the managers of this magnificent Exposition at every stage of its progress. It is a recognition that will do more to cement the friendship of the two races than any occurrence since the dawn of our freedom.

Not only this, but the opportunity here afforded will awaken among us a new era of industrial progress. Ignorant and inexperienced, it is not strange that in the first years of our new life we began at the top instead of at the bottom; that a seat in Congress or the state legislature was more sought than real estate or industrial skill; that the political convention or stump speaking had more attractions than starting a dairy farm or truck garden.

A ship lost at sea for many days suddenly sighted a friendly vessel. From the mast of the unfortunate vessel was seen a signal, "Water, water; we die of thirst!" The answer from the friendly vessel at once came back, "Cast down your bucket where you are." A second time the signal, "Water, water; send us water!" ran up from the distressed vessel, and was answered, "Cast down your bucket where you are." And a third and fourth signal for water was answered, "Cast down your bucket where you are." The captain of the distressed vessel, at last heeding the injunction, cast down his bucket, and it came up full of fresh, sparkling water from the mouth of the Amazon River. To those of my race who depend on bettering their condition in a foreign land or who underestimate the importance of cultivating friendly relations with the Southern white man, who is their next-door neighbor, I would say: "Cast down your bucket where you are"— cast it down in making friends in every manly way of the people of all races by whom we are surrounded.

Cast it down in agriculture, mechanics, in commerce, in domestic service, and in the professions. And in this connection it is well to bear in mind that whatever other sins the South may be called to bear, when it comes to business, pure and simple, it is in the South that the Negro is given a man's chance in the commercial world, and in nothing is this Exposition more eloquent than in emphasizing this chance. Our greatest danger is that in the great leap from slavery to freedom we may overlook the fact that the masses of us are to live by the productions of our hands, and fail to keep in mind that we shall prosper in proportion as we learn to dignify and glorify common labour, and put brains and skill into the common occupations of life; shall prosper in proportion as we learn to draw the line between the superficial and the substantial, the ornamental gewgaws of life and the useful. No race can prosper till it learns that there is as much dignity in tilling a field as in writing a poem. It is at the bottom of life we must begin, and not at the top. Nor should we permit our grievances to overshadow our opportunities.

To those of the white race who look to the incoming of those of foreign birth and strange tongue and habits for the prosperity of the South, were I permitted I would repeat what I say to my own race, "Cast down your bucket where you are." Cast it down among the eight millions of Negroes whose habits you know, whose fidelity and love you have tested in days when to have proved treacherous meant the ruin of your firesides. Cast down your bucket among these people who have, without strikes and labour wars, tilled your fields, cleared your forests, built your railroads and cities, and brought forth treasures from the bowels of the earth, and helped make possible this magnificent representation of the progress of the South. Casting down your bucket among my people, helping and encouraging them as you are doing on these grounds, and to education of head, hand, and heart, you will find that they will buy your surplus land, make blossom the waste places in your fields, and run your factories. While doing this, you can be sure in the future, as in the past, that you and your families will be surrounded by the most patient, faithful, law-abiding, and unresentful people that the world has seen. As we have proved our loyalty to you in the past, in nursing your children, watching by the sick-bed of your mothers and fathers, and often following them with tear-dimmed eyes to their graves, so in the future, in our humble way, we shall stand by you with a devotion that no foreigner can approach, ready to lay down our lives, if need be, in defense of yours, interlacing our industrial, commercial, civil, and religious life with yours in a way that shall make the interests of both races one. In all things that are purely social we can be as separate as the fingers, yet one as the hand in all things essential to mutual progress.

There is no defense or security for any of us except in the highest intelligence and development of all. If anywhere there are efforts tending to curtail the fullest growth of the Negro, let these efforts be turned into stimulating, encouraging, and making him the most useful and intelligent citizen. Effort or means so invested will pay a thousand per cent interest. These efforts will be twice blessed—blessing him that gives and him that takes. There is no escape through law of man or God from the inevitable:

The laws of changeless justice bind Oppressor with oppressed;

And close as sin and suffering joined we march to fate abreast...

Nearly sixteen millions of hands will aid you in pulling the load upward, or they will pull against you the load downward. We shall constitute one-third and more of the ignorance and crime of the South, or one-third [of] its intelligence and progress; we shall contribute one-third to the business and industrial prosperity of the South, or we shall prove a veritable body of death, stagnating, depressing, and retarding every effort to advance the body politic.

Gentlemen of the Exposition, as we present to you our humble effort at an exhibition of our progress, you must not expect overmuch. Starting thirty years ago with ownership here and there in a few quilts and pumpkins and chickens (gathered from miscellaneous sources), remember the path that has led from these to the inventions and production of agricultural implements, buggies, steam-engines, newspapers, books, statuary, carving, paintings, the management of drug stores and banks, has not been trodden without contact with thorns and thistles. While we take pride in what we exhibit as a result of our independent efforts, we do not for a moment forget that our part in this exhibition would fall far short of your expectations but for the constant help that has come to our educational life, not only from the Southern states, but especially from Northern philanthropists, who have made their gifts a constant stream of blessing and encouragement.

The wisest among my race understand that the agitation of questions of social equality is the extremist folly, and that progress in the enjoyment of all the privileges that will come to us must be the result of severe and constant struggle rather than of artificial forcing. No race that has anything to contribute to the markets of the world is long in any degree ostracized. It is important and right that all privileges of the law be ours, but it is vastly more important that we be prepared for the exercise of these privileges. The opportunity to earn a dollar in a factory just now is worth infinitely more than the opportunity to spend a dollar in an opera-house.

In conclusion, may I repeat that nothing in thirty years has given us more hope and encouragement, and drawn us so near to you of the white race, as this opportunity offered by the Exposition; and here bending, as it were, over the altar that represents the results of the struggles of your race and mine, both starting practically empty-handed three decades ago, I pledge that in your effort to work out the great and intricate problem which God has laid at the doors of the South, you shall have at all times the patient, sympathetic help of my race; only let this be constantly in mind, that, while from representations in these buildings of the product of field, of forest, of mine, of factory, letters, and art, much good will come, yet far above and beyond material benefits will be that higher good, that, let us pray God, will come, in a blotting out of sectional differences and racial animosities and suspicions, in a determination to administer absolute justice, in a willing obedience among all classes to the mandates of law. This, coupled with our material prosperity, will bring into our beloved South a new heaven and a new earth.

Source: Louis R. Harlan, ed., *The Booker T. Washington Papers,* Vol. 3, (Urbana: University of Illinois Press, 1974), 583–587.

About the Author

Sarah Washington O'Neal Rush is the great-granddaughter, and the last born of the 16 great-grandchildren in the fourth generation of Booker T. Washington. She is the founder of the Booker T. Washington Empowerment network (B.T.W.E.N.).

B.T.W.E.N. is a nonprofit organization deigned to carry on the legacy of her great grandfather by helping others to create better life circumstances. She believes assisting to lift disadvantage youth and their families, who struggle in their own effort to lift themselves, is a call on her life.

Sarah is no stranger to beating the odds and overcoming obstacles. At the age of 16 she was lost and confused. By the age of 17, she was living on her own in poverty-stricken, drug infested, high crime projects in East Oakland. Yet, defying stereotypical myths, she earned a Bachelor's degree from St. Mary's College in Business

Management, and her Master's degree in Professional Psychology from J.F.K. University. Sarah chose a career in psychotherapy working with groups, individuals, families, couples, adolescents, and adults.

Her professional career consists of over 20 years of working in business and in the mental health field. Eventually, Sarah mapped out a new plan for herself, which included leaving a 16-year career in Corporate America, to begin to pursue work in public speaking, life coaching, presenting workshops, and writing about what she is truly passionate about—helping others lead positive, productive, and healthy lives.

Currently, Sarah is a powerful motivational speaker. She speaks on self-empowering topics, including: Booker T. Washington and his philosophy, discovering your legacy, and overcoming obstacles. She's given talks to students from the first grade to graduate school, in churches, and for various nonprofit agencies. Sarah is a featured writer, a publisher of empowerment materials, and she has written countless articles on mental health and self-improvement. She has appeared on television, highlighting the achievements of her esteemed great-grandfather. Sarah is also an adjunct professor teaching psychology and humanity courses to undergraduate students.

Sarah currently resides in Northern California with her husband, Anthony W. Rush.

For more information visit BTWEN.org or extraordinarylegacy.net.

1/14/15

CPSIA information can be obtained at www.ICGtesting.com
Printed in the USA
LVOW08s1546241214

420311LV00016B/670/P